IF NOT FOR

ATHLETICS

A COLLECTION OF STORIES THAT DEMONSTRATE
THE POWER AND IMPACT OF SPORTS

BLACK LAKE
PUBLISHING COMPANY

Black Lake Publishing, LLC
102 West Eufaula, Suite 200
Norman, OK 73069

Cover design by Jared Stanley

First edition, June 2017
ISBN: 9781549884221

TABLE OF CONTENTS

FOURTH QUARTER: THE PLATFORM *159*

PREGAME

In 2001 I was fresh out of college, working at an advertising agency in Oklahoma City. I didn't have a design degree but fortunately was able to pick up a thing or two from the talented designers around me. When a graphic design job came open at the University of Oklahoma Athletics Department, I jumped at the opportunity as this was a dream job for me. My office was to be in the very stadium where I'd spent my childhood watching the Sooners play. It was here that I realized I wanted to spend my career working in athletics marketing.

After three years at OU, I started my own company and called it Old Hat. I will be referring to Old Hat here and there because I've spent the majority of the past 13 years of my life either working at or thinking about my company, so it's important that you know what Old Hat is and why it's relevant to this book.

Old Hat is a strategic marketing agency dedicated solely to the athletics industry. Since 2004, we have worked with more than 150 sports organizations in the U.S., Canada and France. Our mission is to drive attendance, increase fundraising (on the collegiate level) and improve the game experience for fans. Old Hat has three divisions: Old Hat Creative, Old Hat Sports Branding and Powerhouse. The "Creative" side has been around since 2004 and is primarily focused on the marketing of collegiate athletics. We launched the sports branding division in 2014 to handle athletic organization rebrands consisting of logos, typefaces, jersey design, etc. And finally,

Powerhouse is a company that handles what we call "environmental graph-ics" or "facility graphics" which are anything that can improve the aesthetics of an arena, stadium, building or campus and extend a university's visual branding to the architectural platform.

I'm including information about my companies here so: 1) you know that when I reference "Old Hat" I'm not just talking about some old dirty ball cap of mine, and 2) you understand that I've spent my entire career working in athletics and that on some level, I might be qualified to write a book about it.

I also want to clarify that while I believe sports is powerful on every level, from little league to professional, most of my career has been spent in collegiate athletics. Therefore, the stories in this book are all from people who have worked in the collegiate ranks and much of my perspective is based on what I have witnessed on the university level.

Unsung Heroes

Sport administrators, for those not familiar with the term, are the un-sung heroes of athletics. They're the sports information guys, collecting sta-tistics during the games to send to media outlets, facilitating interviews of our favorite athletes and coaches and getting articles posted on the team website about the events. They're the marketing and promotions team that write the scripts for the games so the P.A. guy knows when to read certain announcements, the band knows when to go onto the field and the intro video plays at the correct time. They're the fundraising people that go out and get donations to build new facilities and support student-athletes with scholarships. And they're the directors of athletics who do their best to keep it all running smoothly.

No one ever starts as an administrator. In order to have the desire to dedicate yourself to a career in athletics administration, you have to have been so struck by the power of athletics that you dedicate your life to giving back to what has given you so much. Throughout this book, you'll read amazing stories from administrators about the ways athletes, coaches and fans positively impacted them.

Administrators spend their careers doing incredible things from be-hind the scenes. We don't hear enough about the positive influence they have on athletes, coaches and fans. They're not the ones scoring points and they're not the ones calling plays and doing post-game interviews. They're not even the ones standing in the bleachers screaming their heads off.

They're the ones standing quietly off to the side, keeping it all going. Their hours are long and their responsibilities are endless. They're in charge of keeping a few hundred student-athletes on the straight and narrow, they have to run clean programs that follow all the rules and at the same time build winning programs. It's a tough job that takes a special kind of person.

That's exactly why I wanted this book to be a collection of stories from administrators. Fans are going to talk about the power of sports from a fan's perspective. Coaches will talk about it from a coach's perspective. Athletes will… you get the point. Administrators are the one group that pull from all perspectives and whose stories give us the most clear picture of the depth and breadth of the way sports shapes us. So when you're reading these stories, keep in mind that you're not just getting the perspective of athletics administrators. You're getting stories from fans, coaches and athletes who love sports so much, they dedicated their careers to it.

These stories are phenomenal. Hearing them has truly been a life-altering experience for me, as it has made me realize just how important sports is to the fabric of our lives. I am honored and humbled by the opportunity to be the avenue through which these stories will make it into your life and I hope I do them justice.

Fan Survey

In order to gather some fan feedback for various parts of this book, Old Hat conducted a sports fan survey in spring 2017. We sent the survey out to 10,000 people from all over the United States that had previously designated themselves as sports fans. We wanted all age groups, genders, socioeconomic backgrounds and geographic locations represented.

Most of the relevant data from this report will be found in my commentary throughout this book. However, if you would like to view an infographic of the survey results, you may do so at: http://oldhatcreative.com/blog/heres-what-sports-fans-really-think

The Stories

While my name is on the cover of this book, this would not have been possible without the contributions of the numerous athletic administrators who shared their stories. Rather than simply interview these administrators and use their feedback to help craft the direction of the message, I thought it only fair to share their stories as they told them. For the record, every single one of these stories was provided to me via a recorded phone conversation.

We then transcribed each conversation and created a narrative around the story they told. We submitted the stories to each participant with the instruction that they had 100% editorial control over the story and that we wouldn't print a word of it without their go-ahead. It was important to me that we got their story right and I felt that the only way to do that was to: 1) let each one of them edit their own story as they saw fit and 2) only print what they approved.

I also think it's important to note (and this speaks to the power of the subject matter of this book) that I ended up asking 59 administrators to participate in this book. You can flip through the pages of this book and count the names of the people you see, or you can just trust me when I tell you that of those 59 requests, 57 of them agreed to participate. And it's also important to point out that not a single person was compensated in any way for their time or story. They simply wanted to do it because they believed in the importance of this message.

As a thank you to all those who have participated, I will be donating a portion of any profits from the sale of this book to a general athletic scholarship fund. One of the most important themes in this book is the power sports has to educate student-athletes, many of whom would never have had access to an education otherwise. I hope this book helps promote that idea both through its message and through a financial contribution to that fund.

The Podcast

After listening to story after story and realizing how great they are, I decided to turn some of them into a podcast series. The name of the podcast is *Stop the Clock* and it is available on iTunes and Google Play. So if you'd like to hear some of the stories as told by the individual who lived them, give the podcast a listen. Follow me on Twitter @ZacLogsdon for up-to-date news on new episodes being released and other information about *If Not for Athletics* and *Stop the Clock*.

FIRST QUARTER
THE BOOK

There I was, traveling 70 mph while strapped to a four-thousand-foot hunk of steel, heading down the backside of a 145-foot vertical loop. But for some reason, I couldn't stop thinking about something totally unrelated to the Superman: Krypton Coaster I was being whipped around on. It was spring break and my wife and I had taken our four children to Six Flags Fiesta Texas in San Antonio. It was kinda cold that morning and a light rain had started right after we walked in the gates. So in addition to being a little cold and a little wet… and a little nauseous… I was traveling like a speeding bullet around this thing, and the thing that kept running through my mind: *Sports.*

That's right. I was on vacation, hundreds of miles from home, riding on a roller coaster and I couldn't stop myself from pondering the question of, *I wonder what percentage of people at the amusement park are wearing sports team apparel.* All day as we were walking past the funnel cake stands and Looney Tunes characters, I was making mental notes of how many people I saw wearing sports team apparel. I lost count pretty quickly but rest assured that it was a lot. Whether it was their high school volleyball team practice shirt, a Texas Longhorns shirt or a University of Tennessee at Chattanooga ball cap, everyone seemed to be wearing something advertising their favorite sports team.

I was trying to pay close attention so I could get an actual percentage estimate of sports team apparel versus non-sports apparel. But I'd be lying if I said I was able to do so. However, I would say that a conservative estimate is that one-third of the people I saw there were wearing at least one article of clothing that was representative of a sports team. Heck, I was a part of that group too. I was the guy in the Chattanooga hat (Go Mocs!) and I was also wearing my "The Boz" t-shirt.

So of the 20,000 people at Six Flags that day, roughly 7,000 of them were wearing sports team apparel. The important thing to note about that though is that it's not like the other two-thirds were wearing clothing promoting *their* favorite form of entertainment. I didn't see one-third in sports team apparel, one-third in movie-themed t-shirts and one-third in shirts promoting those people's favorite bands. No, as a matter of fact, I saw one person wearing a movie t-shirt, one person in a band t-shirt and the rest were pretty much in either generic clothing with nothing on it (or just a brand name) or, you guessed it, sports team apparel.

Why is that? Why do we love sports so much that we're willing to adorn ourselves from head to toe in clothing that advertises a team, with absolutely no payback at all? We fill our closets with all this expensive apparel that promotes our favorite sports teams and then we go spend even more money to watch those teams play. And we're thrilled to do it!

But *why*? Why do we do this? What is it about sports that affects us so drastically that we give our hearts and souls and hard-earned cash over to it without blinking an eye?

It's because sports permeates everything we do and enhances our lives in ways most of us never think about. What I aim to do with this book is bring all of those things to light through the stories I've been told from men and women who have dedicated their careers to athletics.

If Not for Athletics is a collection of 64 stories from 57 athletics administrators from athletic organizations all across the country. In collecting these stories, I noticed they all seemed to fall into one of three major categories. The book is divided into four quarters. The first quarter is about this book, why I wrote it, why it needed to be written and a little bit about my background. The subsequent three quarters contain stories from each of the three categories.

Welcome to the First Quarter of *If Not for Athletics*.

❶
CHAPTER ONE
KICKOFF

> ❝ **If** there is a book that you want to read, but it hasn't been written yet, you must be the one to write it. ❞
>
> *- Toni Morrison*

Kirby Puckett.

That's where I parked earlier this week at the airport parking garage. Last time, it was Larry Bird. I park in Brian Bosworth as often as possible, because he's my all-time favorite college football player, but technically, a spot in Spencer Tillman is better. It's impossible to find a spot in Magic Johnson or Jackie Robinson because they're closest. But anything is better than Junior Seau.

See, the parking garage I use at the Oklahoma City airport has 5 floors and 3 stations. Station 3, floor 2 is pretty much the closest you can hope to find a spot. Station 5 is farthest from the terminal and floor 5 is up on the roof so your car is exposed to the elements if you park there. But I'm terrible at remembering which station and floor I'm parked on because I travel so much for work. Is it station 3, floor 4? Or station 4, floor 3?! I can never remember.

So I do what I'm sure a lot of us do. I remember the name of an athlete that wore that number. Station 3, floor 2... that's Magic Johnson. Recently I was traveling with Deb, a colleague of mine, and when we arrived back in OKC and were walking to our cars, I said, *Larry Bird*. She looked at me like I was nuts (which is a look I'm accustomed to from her) and said, *Uh, what?*

Larry Bird. 33. That's where I'm parked.

She understood. So when I parked in station 3, on floor 4 the following week and no one was coming to mind, I sent a quick email to Deb and she helped me out.

Kirby Puckett, she said.

When I returned back to Oklahoma City I texted her.

Me: *Kirby Puckett.*
Deb: *You're in 34.*
Me: *(thumbs up emoji)*

This is nothing new for me. This is also how I used to remember my school locker combinations. Mookie Blaylock, Willie Mays, Babe Ruth. If you want to break into my locker on the first floor of Guthrie Jr. High School, that's all you have to remember.

These are examples of how sports permeates everything we do. I work in sports and have every day of my life for nearly two decades. But I'm confident even those of you who have never worked in sports may do the exact same thing when you park at airports or remember locker combinations. If we think about it, there are countless ways that sports affects our everyday lives.

How much of your wardrobe is sports team apparel? How much leisure time do you spend watching sports, whether it's college, professional or your daughter's club volleyball team? How much time did you spend planning your Super Bowl party or figuring out where you were going to watch the game? How much time do you spend talking about sports, attending sporting events, watching SportsCenter, reading *The Sporting News* or playing fantasy football?

I'm sure your answer to at least one of these questions is: *A lot.*

Sports has an amazing impact on our lives. Whether we play it, coach it, work in it or just watch it, sports touches everything we do. And I firmly believe there's no one thing we do that has a more positive impact on as many aspects of our lives. Sports influenced me so much that I have spent my career trying to increase attendance at sporting events. I have hundreds and hundreds of amazing memories surrounding sporting events and it occurred to me that if my great sports experiences drove me to a career in athletics, there must be many others who have similar experiences. I thought about how much I'd like to hear a story about a time when people like Barry Alvarez, Joe Castiglione and Tom Osborne witnessed the true power and impact of athletics. I knew that if I have some really great stories to tell, theirs would put mine to shame.

I thought, *Someone should put together a book of those stories because that's something I'd love to read.* Shortly after, I decided that person should be me.

The idea came to me in November of 2016. Three months later, I had compiled 64 stories from 57 athletic directors and senior administrators from universities all over the United States. As you will see, I was right about the stories. They are truly amazing examples of the power and impact sports has on us. Better yet, these stories are inspirational to anyone involved in sports in any way. Whether you're an administrator, coach, athlete or fan, the positive impact that you can have on the lives of others cannot be overstated. This book should serve as a great way to remind us all of how our small role in sports is part of a much larger picture and that without all of us, sports would not have the far-reaching impact it does.

My hope is that you're now thinking one of two things: 1) You know exactly what I'm talking about and are excited to see what's in store in the pages ahead or 2) I'm nuts and that *it's just a game,* which is what my mom used to say to me when I was furious over a huge loss. For that second group, I'm even more excited for you to read this book. Because it's not just a game. It's so much more. If not for athletics, we would miss out on so many things we take for granted. I hope this book convinces you and my mom of that. More importantly, I hope after reading this book you view athletics through a new lens and have a greater appreciation for the way sports shapes our lives.

So this is *If Not for Athletics*, a collection of stories from men and women that have dedicated their careers to athletics because they have seen firsthand the many ways in which sports enriches our lives.

2
CHAPTER TWO
MANIFESTO

My greatest memories as a kid were playing sports with my dad and watching sports with my dad.

- Mark Teixeira

Thanks, Craig

Many years ago, my older brother Craig came to me with an idea to compile a book for my dad of our greatest sports moments with him. So that's just what we did. I designed a logo for it and we put together a 30-or-so page book of some of the greatest memories we had with him. Other family members contributed too and we ended up with a great collection of fun memories to give him. We gave him the book for Christmas that year and I don't think I've ever seen him as emotional as he was when he opened it. Those memories meant the world to us and I realized that day that they meant just as much to him.

I think that was the first time I realized the impact sports has on people. My brother opened the door for me to see how powerful memories can be. I believe that, subconsciously, that's when I decided to pursue a career that put me in a position to help create those memories for other people.

Two months later, I took a job as a graphic designer for the University of Oklahoma Athletics Department and began my career in athletics.

The Old Hat Manifesto

I'm including this so you can more fully understand my perspective on the power of sports and why I'm writing this book. It's also to set the stage for what's to come after, where I admit that I didn't fully understand a thing or two about the impact of sports. But I don't want to ruin it for you so that's all I'll say for now.

What you're about to read is the *Old Hat Manifesto*. This is why I do what I do and why I feel it's important.

My father cried on November 16, 1957. He was 12 years old and he wept on my grandfather's lap as he had just experienced something he had no recollection of ever having experienced before. His beloved Oklahoma Sooners lost a football game for the first time in more than 4 years. When OU began their 47-game winning streak, he was only 8 years old. So there he sat, tears flowing down his cheeks, while his father held him and assured him that everything would be okay.

Twenty-five years later, my father passed along his love of the Sooners to me. On Saturday afternoons in the early 1980s, he and I would get in the car and leave our farmhouse in Guthrie, Oklahoma for the hour drive to Norman. Going to OU football games was not guaranteed but often I would have begged enough that my dad would give in and take me. Sometimes the whole family. Sometimes just me. We'd stop by the tailgate of James and Maryanna Martin for fried chicken. We'd go watch The Pride of Oklahoma (OU's marching band) warm up. We'd throw a football around on the South Oval. And I would bring every dollar I had saved so I could buy a new OU jersey at the stadium. But the best part was sitting next to my dad while he explained the finer points of the game of football to me.

Those memories and so many like them are some of the greatest moments from my childhood. In all of them, I remember who I was with, what I was wearing and most importantly, I remember the emotions I felt. I remember where I was when the Denver Broncos won their first Super Bowl. I remember night after night at the Lloyd Noble Center with my brother and dad watching Wayman, Mookie, Tim and Stacey play basketball. I remember a flyover at the old Mile High Stadium before the game started and how loud and overwhelming it was. I remember meeting Ozzie Smith in the parking garage outside Busch Stadium and getting him to sign a ball for me before we took in an afternoon Cardinals game. I remember standing next to Zac Stevens in Oklahoma Memorial Stadium as the clock wound down after OU beat #1 Nebraska 31-14 after spending years in that same stadium as students watching OU lose game after game after game.

I remember, because those moments are important. I remember, because now that I am older and my brother has moved a thousand miles away, Zac Stevens and I rarely make time for each other and I don't see my father nearly as much as I should, those moments are what I hold as my most prized possessions. No one can take them from me and I'll take those memories to my grave.

These are the moments that sports creates. Sports brings people together and creates moments shared by fathers and sons, mothers and daughters, brothers and sisters, and friends. I've never met anyone, regardless of how much of a sports fan they are, who doesn't have at least one great memory surrounding a sporting event. They remember where they were, who they were with and what happened at that event that made it so special. Chances are, they get emotional when they think about these experiences. I get emotional just talking about it. Some people have one. Some people have many. I'm lucky... I have hundreds.

Sports are important, plain and simple. Sporting events provide an avenue for people to have experiences that shape their lives. Sports gives people memories that stay with them til the day they die. More often than not, even when their team lost, the memory is held as a fond one.

Sporting events are in a battle with convenience. And the statistics show that we are losing. Kids are upstairs in their rooms playing video games or texting their friends while dad is downstairs in his man cave binge-watching Netflix. When that child is 80 years old, they aren't going to be telling their grandchildren about the Saturday afternoons they spent playing video games. But being outside on a Saturday afternoon with thousands of other people screaming for the same cause, a ballpark hot dog in their hands while sitting next to the people they care about most? That creates a memory that will live on forever.

Old Hat's mission is to help create those moments for people.

I believe that there's nothing greater than sharing a sports experience with someone you care about. I also believe that the purity of these moments is being lost to technology and convenience. Too often *families opt to stay at home, everyone in separate rooms of the house staring at their own devices and not connecting with one another. My son will have no memory of the Saturday afternoon he spent playing Minecraft while I watched Breaking Bad on Netflix. However, he still remembers going to the OU vs. Texas football game when he was only 8 years old. He doesn't remember if OU won or lost. He remembers that he was with his brother and his dad. He will always remember it. Because of the experience.*

I wrote the Old Hat Manifesto to both inform our clients and potential clients what our company stands for but also as a call-to-arms for the Old Hat staff. It was this manifesto that was the inspiration for me to write this book. And as I said, I thought that if I had all of these amazing memories about great moments in sports and the way it brought people together, surely everyone else who had dedicated their lives to a career in sports would have similar stories. They'd have some great memory about a specific event and how it created such a passion in them that they had no choice but to seek out a career in athletics.

Boy, was I wrong.

I've been wrong about many things in my life. But I'm not sure I've ever missed the mark as badly as I did when I made this assumption about the people I'd be interviewing for this book. Don't misunderstand me though. I wasn't wrong in the sense that they didn't have amazing stories to tell. Or that they didn't understand the power of sports.

No, it was I who didn't understand. I had no idea how powerful sports is and all the ways it shapes our lives. My understanding was too limited. To me, sports was important simply because of the memories created in those moments. Of course, I knew there was more to it than that. I knew there were other powerful reasons why people love sports. What I didn't know was just how far-reaching the impact is.

I've always known that if not for athletics, we'd miss out on so many of life's most influential moments. But until I started writing this book, I had absolutely no idea how true that is.

③

CHAPTER THREE
BLOCK THAT KICK

"Do you know what my favorite part of the game is? The opportunity to play."
- Mike Singletary

The Sooners trailed the Buckeyes 26 to 28 with 6 seconds left in the game. All it would take is a 41-yard field goal by OU kicker Uwe von Shamann to win the game. Von Shamann was 5-for-5 on the season but 41-yards was no "gimme." Not to mention he was in enemy territory. That September day in 1977, OU was playing *in* Columbus with the legendary Woody Hayes leading the Buckeyes from the opposing sideline. Nearly 90,000 fans, most of whom were Buckeye fans, were cheering for this 21-year-old kid to fail at the only job he was placed on the field to do. The pressure was on.

OU had called a timeout to set up for the attempt. Uwe stretched, took a moment to focus, lined up for the kick and just as the ball was about to be snapped: Timeout, Ohio State.

Ohio State wanted Uwe to think about that kick a little bit longer. Any football fan knows this is a popular tactic known as "icing" the kicker. The idea is to let the kicker get nervous. To make him think about it a little longer and maybe, just maybe, make it more likely that he'll miss. When you're the home team, you get the added bonus of having thousands of fans trying to get in the kicker's head. And that's exactly what the Buckeye fans did.

The Sooners went to the sideline during the timeout. As they returned to the field and von Shamann strapped his helmet back on, the Buckeye faithful could be heard chanting, *Block that kick! Block that kick!*

Imagine being 21 years old and about to attempt a 41-yard field goal to beat one of the historical powerhouses of college football, in one of the most fabled stadiums in the country, against a legendary coach, as the visiting team, while 80,000+ people are screaming for you to fail and thousands of others are hoping beyond all hope that you'll make it. Would you let it get to you?

Uwe von Shamann didn't. Or if he did, he certainly didn't let it show. Rather than freeze under the pressure, von Shamann did something he's still known for 40 years later. He began directing the chant. He put his hands up like a conductor in an orchestra as if he were leading the chant himself.

What happened next is known as "The Kick." Von Shamann did what he had done so many times. He lined up, the ball was snapped and he kicked it through the uprights. Final score, OU - 29, Ohio State - 28.

Von Shamann had the weight of the world on his shoulders in those moments. But rather than let it get to him, he embraced it. He realized how fortunate he was to be in that moment. Some people in that position would have thought about how many people were screaming at them to fail. Uwe thought about how many people had faith that he'd succeed. Some people would let the fact that they were in enemy territory get to them. Uwe just thought about how lucky he was to be able to compete in such a great game.

Be the Conductor

Years ago, when I was developing Old Hat's guiding principles, I wanted to make the point to our staff that sometimes we're under a lot of pressure to deliver on tight deadlines. Sometimes clients are pushing us to do the impossible. Our competitors are hoping we'll fail. In those moments, when we're working long hours, dealing with less-than-admirable circumstances, we have to take a timeout, look around us and realize how lucky we are to be doing what we're doing. When every voice is screaming, *Block that kick,* we have to turn around and direct them in their chant. We have to smile in their faces because we get to be in that moment. We get to work in sports day in and day out. We get to make videos that play in front of millions of fans, posters that hang in kids' bedrooms and websites that help promote sports initiatives. We get to do what a lot of people dream of doing. We must remind ourselves, like Uwe did, of how lucky we are.

I bring this story up because I heard this same idea coming through in nearly every conversation I had with the athletic directors and senior staff members who provided stories for this book. The stories they told that illustrated their particular view on the power and impact of sports didn't pertain to this idea, but time and time again, they told me they felt extremely lucky to have the opportunity to do the job they do. They weren't just speaking about this from an administrator's standpoint. Everyone I spoke to started out as a fan, athlete and/or coach. Yet despite different perspectives, every story shared the same underlying theme: *We are so lucky to be in the position we're in.*

The thing to remember though is that when the pressure is on and the weight of the world is on your shoulders, just turn around and be the conductor. When everyone is screaming at you to fail, think about everyone who is pulling for you to succeed. When your team is on the losing end of that 41-yard kick, consider how fortunate you are to have been able to witness it. When everyone is yelling, *Block that kick,* look them straight in the eye, raise your hands, and direct them in it.

We are so lucky to be able to be involved in the sports experience, whether we are a fan, coach, athlete or administrator. Sports does more good for more people than any other pastime or form of entertainment. It educates, it builds character, it influences, it heals… the list goes on and on. We get to be a part of it!

SECOND QUARTER
THE EVENT

As the 1969 football season came to a close, the nation's top two teams were the Texas Longhorns in the No. 1 spot and the Arkansas Razorbacks at No. 2. Both had won a national championship in the sixties and were coached by legends of the game, Darrell Royal and Frank Broyles, respectively. They had also completely dominated the Southwest Conference over the previous decade, one of the two having won the conference title eight of the previous 10 years. So on December 6, when the Longhorns went to Razorback Stadium to figure out who the number one team in the country really was, all eyes were on Fayetteville.

As you can imagine, the hype around the game was unbelievable. This was the 100th year of college football and Texas had won 18 games straight. Richard Nixon, president at the time, attended the game with then-Texas U.S. Representative George H.W. Bush. Nixon even announced that the winner would receive a plaque declaring them the National Champions.

The game was one for the ages as Arkansas dominated the first 3 quarters. The Longhorns turned the ball over 6 times and were unable to score a single point. The score with only one quarter left to play: Arkansas 14, Texas 0. But the fourth quarter was a different story altogether. Texas scored on the first play and followed it with a successful 2-point conversion making the score 14-8. The Razorbacks answered right back by driving 73 yards to the Texas 7-yard-line before an interception in the end zone thwarted Arkansas' attempt to cushion their lead. Texas responded with an 80-yard drive resulting in a touchdown and extra point, and Arkansas threw another interception on their next drive, ending their hopes for a victory.

Final score: Texas 15, Arkansas 14

Arkansas fans who were alive back then remember that game well. I know this, because a 10-year-old boy named Matt was at that game. Matt is 57 now and he told me the story of that game while sitting next to me on an airplane. He told the story with such passion and excitement, I felt like I was there. I felt the pain he went through seeing his Razorbacks lose that game. I felt it because I've felt that same pain so many times as a sports fan. My favorite part of that story, though, is that of all the stories he could have told me, he told me one about a heartbreaking loss. But he wasn't angry or bitter about it. He told it with a smile on his face. He remembered that day fondly because it was a great moment in sports for him. Forty-seven years later and he's able to see just how fortunate he was to have witnessed that game.

That's one of the most powerful things sports does. Not only does it create moments that a 57-year-old man still remembers vividly, it connects people in a way that no other thing can. Sports takes two strangers on an airplane and it gives them something to talk about. It connects us because we've all been there at some point and felt those emotions. We relate to each other's exciting stories about big wins and empathize with the pain felt in stories of gut-wrenching losses.

So much of this book is about the ancillary benefits of sports – its power to heal, influence, build relationships and so many other things that happen outside the lines on a playing field. However, we must not forget that none of it would be possible without all of the things that happen inside those lines.

That's what this section is about. Last-second wins, pregame traditions, underdog stories and the crazy things we do to help our team to victory. But first, let's talk about losing.

4

CHAPTER FOUR
WINNING ISN'T EVERYTHING

❝ **I've learned that something constructive comes from every defeat.** ❞

- Tom Landry

I've always been a huge fan of the Oklahoma Sooners. Attending Sooner football games was the highlight of my childhood and I particularly enjoyed watching us beat Oklahoma State year after year after year. In fact, when I was 18 years old, the Sooners hadn't lost to Oklahoma State in football in my entire life. That was 1995 and the last time the Cowboys had beaten the Sooners was the year before I was born, 1976. Eighteen years of dominance that as far as I knew would continue until I died an old man. But on this cool November afternoon, Howard Schnellenberger's Sooners didn't just lose to Oklahoma State. They were completely shut out. Twelve to zero.

Everything I knew about the world was suddenly in question. I was a bit concerned that the earth was going to spin off its axis. Because there is a list of irrefutable laws of physics and at the very top of that list it clearly states: Oklahoma does not lose to Oklahoma State in football. But that day, the laws of physics did not apply. And the most gut-wrenching loss of my life wrenched my gut something awful. I couldn't speak. I couldn't eat. I just went home and took a nap.

Eighteen years of winning made that loss nearly impossible to stomach. But what if we'd lost the year before? Would losing in 1995 have hurt as badly? Of course not. If we had lost 9 times out of those 18 years would losing in 1995 have been so devastating? Most definitely not. The more you lose, the less it hurts. Just ask Oklahoma State fans. They endured 18 consecutive losses. Think another one would have hurt as badly as it did for OU fans to endure their first in nearly two decades?

Sports teaches us so many things about life. But possibly the most valuable lesson it teaches is how to lose. Life is full of loss. We face it every day. The pain when our favorite team comes up short often pales in comparison to the other losses that life brings us. But we lose every day in one way or another. Every day, we fail at something. If not for athletics, we wouldn't have that experience of picking ourselves up, dusting ourselves off and trying again. Whether we're playing in the game as an athlete, watching from the stands or participating as an administrator, losses teach us way more about life than wins ever could.

Chapter 4 is about times when people saw the power and impact that sports can have even when their team didn't win. Keep in mind that I was asking these people to share a great moment in sports when they saw just how powerful sports can be and these were the first things that came to mind for them. So if you work in sports and you think that winning is the most important factor to creating great moments in sports, these stories from your peers would indicate otherwise. If you're a fan, I hope that you'll read these stories and realize that great moments in sports don't only happen when your team wins. It's about so much more than that.

THE BATTLE
AT BRISTOL

• • • • • • •

WHIT BABCOCK
Athletic Director
Virginia Tech

Almost equidistant between Blacksburg, VA and Knoxville, TN stands the town of Bristol. The Virginia-Tennessee state line actually runs along the center of Main Street there. Virginia Tech and the University of Tennessee are both about 120 miles away from Bristol, which made it the perfect location for a unique rivalry game event between the two programs.

Planning for the Battle at Bristol took years, and I came into my current position at Virginia Tech just in time to experience the event itself. My predecessor Jim Weaver helped set up the game. From the very beginning, the goal was to try to break the all-time college football attendance record. Prior to the Battle at Bristol, the record was 115,109 attendees at a 2013 Michigan-Notre Dame game. On September 10, 2016 we blew that record out of the water with 156,990 people in the stands at Bristol Motor Speedway. We even surpassed the NFL's highest attendance record!

Coming into that game was like what you'd imagine Woodstock to have been. There were people everywhere. As you walked up to the stadium, there were fans as far as the eye could see. And it wasn't just fans of our two teams: the word had gotten out that we were making this a once-in-a-lifetime event, so a lot of the people came to the game just because they were fans of college football and wanted to be part of something special.

The pageantry of that game was unbelievable. Kenny Chesney hosted a concert at the track the night before the game; Jennifer Nettles of Sugarland sang the National Anthem; Peyton Manning and Bruce Smith participated in the coin toss ceremony as alumni of Tennessee and Virginia Tech respectively; and a representative from Guinness World Records presented a plaque recognizing the Battle of Bristol as the largest American college football game ever. From watching all the work behind the scenes to seeing years of planning come together for the game itself, it was an incredible experience. The crowds, the flashing lights, the patriotism and just the feeling you got standing on the field… it was unbelievable. To me, it was bigger than even the Super Bowl. It was just this perfect storm celebrating college football.

Virginia Tech started strong with a 14-0 lead during the first quarter but we ended up losing the game 45-24. Even though we lost, that game was a truly memorable experience. One of our offensive lineman, Jonathan McLaughlin, really captured it in some of the things he said after the game was over. He talked about how it had been an experience he would never forget and he knew someday he would be telling his grandkids about it.

I think that's one of the things sports teaches young people: how to win with class and lose with dignity. You can't always win; that's just real life. And with sports, everybody sees it when you have a bad day. Winning isn't always the most important thing. It's the lessons you learn, the experiences you have and the memories you make. Sure, it would have been great to win college football's biggest game ever. But the thing our players and all those fans will remember for the rest of their lives is the incredible experience they had being part of the Battle at Bristol. It's something they'll never forget. Nor will I.

EACH OTHER

• • • • • • •

MICHAEL BEALE
Assistant Athletic Director
University of North Carolina

Over the past couple of years, I have been very fortunate to work as an administrator for the volleyball program at the University of North Carolina. Two of their last four seasons have come to an end at the University of Minnesota during the NCAA tournament.

The setup at the University of Minnesota is kind of unique. The players have to go down the stairs after leaving the court only to have to come back up to the court to walk across the hall to the interview room. Watching those young women come back up and walk across the court after a loss is just heartbreaking. The freshmen are kind of shell-shocked, like they can't grasp what just happened, but you can tell they're already thinking, *Okay, we'll get back here again.* The seniors are visibly in pain as they realize their playing career has come to an end. They're saying things like, *I can't believe it's over. I don't ever want to take my uniform off.* But as they're walking off the court with tears in their eyes, they have their arms around each other. They're still in it together, and you can just tell there's a bond and a sisterhood there that will last a lifetime.

That, along with seeing the reactions from the parents and family members, is the most moving part for me. It was close to midnight when all was said and done, yet the parents and family members were still waiting in the arena. As the girls came up and walked across the court, everyone started clapping for them and hugging them. Players and families were crying and embracing in this overwhelming mix of pain, love, and support. Even coaches who don't normally ever show emotion were breaking down because it was such a great group of girls. Being there for that moment was one of the most gut-wrenching experiences I've ever had.

The younger players could have gone back to the hotel while the seniors completed their interviews, but every single one of those kids decided to wait. They were like, *We came over together and we're going back together.* They didn't care how late it was or that it was freezing outside and only getting colder the longer they waited. They were going back to the hotel together as a team no matter what and were going to be a team to the very end.

As much as you hate to see your players suffer the pain of losing, seeing their resilience and the strength of their bond is inspiring. It was incredibly moving to see how much the concept of being a team meant to them. Even in that moment of extreme disappointment, they were able to recognize that they hadn't lost the most important part of the game: each other.

HOT DOG NIGHT

• • • • • • •

KIM RECORD
Director of Athletics
University of North Carolina at Greensboro (UNCG)

In 1986, Virginia had a really good women's basketball team. Even though they were ranked third in the nation, our average attendance at games was only about 300 people. At that time schools didn't spend a lot of money marketing women's basketball but our Associate AD, Todd Turner, and I came up with this idea that we were going to set an attendance record at our upcoming game against No. 15 ranked UNC Chapel Hill, who was our nemesis.

We started kicking around ideas with our coach Debbie Ryan and others. They helped us brainstorm ways to get as many people as possible to the game and we decided to pull out all the stops. We came up with a plan to donate money to a charity based on the number of people who attended the game, and we lined up some sponsors so we could give away a free hot dog and a Coke to anyone who showed up. *Come to Hot Dog Night!* We even offered free game tickets just to get people there. To get the media excited, we created a halftime event that pitted print writers versus television writers. We turned that rivalry game into a really big deal and we marketed the heck out of it!

I remember getting a call from our ticket people (who were in California for a conference) just a couple of days before the event. They had a conflict and weren't going to be able to be there. I said to them, *Then who's going to be here when all these people are coming in?* They were like, *Kim, it's not going to be that big. You're going to have a thousand people tops.* I wasn't convinced, because I knew how hard we'd been pushing the game. So I talked to Todd about the ticket people being out of town. I kept saying, *I'm telling you I really think this is going to be a big crowd! We need to have more ushers. We're not prepared!* Todd didn't believe me either. He just laughed and said, *If we fill this building I'll dance naked at halftime.*

We had really created a buzz and everybody around town was talking about Hot Dog Night. The day of the game, people started to line up outside the arena at eight o'clock in the morning. When I saw that happening, I got really excited and started saying to my co-workers, *People are lining up already! I'm telling you, we're going to do this!* And everyone else in the department was looking at me going, *You're crazy, Kim.* As game time approached and we opened the doors, we were overrun with people. There was no way to tell who had bought tickets in advance and who had just shown up. It was such an unexpectedly large crowd that we had no idea what to do. In the end, we let all of them in.

The final attendance count for Hot Dog Night set a record at 11,174. It was incredible! Our building wasn't even designed to hold that many people, it was only supposed to hold 9,000 officially. But we didn't care – we just kept letting people in. It got so crowded that you couldn't walk through the concourse to get a hot dog. That was probably a good thing, because we hadn't been sophisticated enough to put a limit on the giveaways. The place was completely packed and it was amazing. Everywhere you looked that night, you saw fans: in the aisles, behind the baskets, up near the rafters. The fire marshal came and he wasn't too happy, but I was overjoyed. We had done it!

Going into that game, we had a 20-0 record and everyone thought for certain we would win it. But both teams played their hearts out and it ended up being a tight game. The arena got stiflingly hot with so many extra people in the stands and the noise was deafening as the lead went back and forth. In the end, we lost 60-58 on a buzzer beater. I was devastated. We had put so much work into it and I remember sort of sitting there, wanting to cry. Although it was a really tough loss, Coach Debbie Ryan stepped up and handled things graciously. She took a few minutes to thank the crowd for coming and making it such a great event.

When I was able to take a step back and think about it, I realized that

Coach Ryan was right. Even though we lost the game, that night was an incredible victory for our marketing team and for the women's basketball program. Hot Dog Night is a moment that will live on in Virginia Basketball history forever. It was an unbelievable game and an unbelievable experience for our team and for our fans.

WIDE RIGHT

• • • • • • •

MARK RIORDAN
*Vice President of Marketing and Communications
for the 12th Man Foundation*
Texas A&M University

I grew up in western New York, about an hour south of Rich Stadium where the Buffalo Bills played. People wanted to root for the Bills because they were the hometown team, but in the '80s that was tough because the Bills were horrible. There weren't really any college teams nearby that we could call our own, so we rooted for the Bills anyway.

Everyone around there always said the Bills were their team, but everyone I knew also picked another team to root for. It was just too thankless being purely a Bills fan. There were a lot of Cleveland Browns fans, Pittsburgh fans, Dallas Cowboys fans, and Broncos fans. I picked several teams to root for over the years. I was a San Diego Chargers fan at one point; then I was a Philadelphia Eagles fan because Ron Jaworski was the quarterback and I liked the fact that his nickname was the Polish Rifle and that he was from Buffalo.

My freshman year in high school, it seemed like things were going to change for the Bills so I committed 100% to being a Bills fan. I started telling my buddies, *The Bills are going to come around. They've got this. They just got this running back, I watched him in preseason, he's awesome, his name's Thurman Thomas.* I remember having that conversation at the Burger King in town after going to the movies and everyone was just like, *Whatever Mark.* My friends would talk about how the Bills weren't for real, but I didn't care. I had bought in.

The Bills had a slow couple of years, but then in the 1990 season everything started clicking. They had a lot of big names on the team and they just kept getting better. There were all the Buffalo songs like, *The Bills make me want to shout!*, and the *Respect* song, you know, like *R-E-S-P-E-C-T, Jim Kelly passed to Andre Reed.* Suddenly everyone was jumping on the bandwagon. People were getting frenzied because they're winning, they're winning, they're winning! The Bills made it to the AFC Championship game that season. My buddy Frank and I managed to get tickets to the game for $50 each and it was awesome! I can remember everything about that game. The Bills dominated the Raiders and won 51-3. That should be the moment I'm talking about, but it's not.

The next game for the Bills was the Super Bowl. It was my senior year of high school, and it was like every dream that I'd had for the Bills the last three years was coming to fruition. On Super Bowl Sunday, we were at my friend JP's house and six or seven of us were piled into his bedroom watching the game. It was going back and forth and back and forth, the Bills would take control, then the Giants would take control. There was a point where I thought, *It's going to happen. It's just going to happen.* It came down to the end and we were on the edges of our seats. There were about eight seconds left and the Bills line up for a 47-yard field goal. Scott Norwood came up to take the kick. The tension was unbelievable.

I remember getting on my knees in front of the TV with a couple of other guys and watching the snap, watching the kick, then watching it push wide right. To this day, if you say, *wide right* to a Buffalo Bills fan - and probably any football fan - they immediately think of Scott Norwood.

I fell face first onto the floor with tears in my eyes. For about ten or fifteen minutes after the game ended, we all just kind of sat there staring off into space in disbelief. We were in complete shock. How could this have happened? Nobody should have beaten that awesome, high-powered Bills team! They should have crushed the Giants. But they didn't, and I might have been a high school senior but I wanted to cry like a baby. I was absolutely devastated.

My first three years of college were dictated by the Bills making the Super Bowl and thinking each year, *this is the year.* Except every year, it wasn't. They lost to the Redskins, then they lost to the Cowboys, and then they lost to the Cowboys again. Every time, it was like a punch in the stomach. Those three Super Bowl losses didn't hurt nearly as much as the first one, but they still hurt. I gave up after a while. It was just too hard to keep pulling for the Bills, only to be let down again and again.

Even so, the Bills are still part of my identity. To this day, if somebody asks, *Where are you from?* I'll say, *Buffalo.* I'm not from Buffalo; I'm from an hour-and-a-half south of Buffalo. Sometimes I wonder: *What if the Bills had won one or even all four of those Super Bowls? Would I have a different outlook on thinking, Of course we're going to win?* That experience definitely shaped my view of sports, and because of it I've put everything I have into working with NCAA football. I know that even when we're thinking this could be the year and we get kicked in the gut, I can help them get through it.

DEALERS IN HOPE

• • • • • • •

BRAD WURTHMAN
Senior Associate Athletics Director,
External Operations
Virginia Tech

Growing up in Hamilton, Ontario really meant growing up in the shadow of Toronto. Hamilton is the grit to Toronto's white-collar. For those who aren't familiar with the area, the reality is that Hamilton is "the little brother" but it's still a really large city in its own right. It's one of the ten largest cities in Canada, but it gets no love from anyone because it's a blue-collar steel town that was built on the backs of union laborers and workers. At one point Hamilton had two of the world's three largest steel mills but as production and manufacturing slowed, those industries slowed along with my city.

Toronto had the Maple Leafs, the Blue Jays and the Raptors, and we loved them all, but Hamilton had the Tiger-Cats. That's the team I grew up rooting for and they're the DNA of that community. It's not that I don't love Toronto too, but I was born and raised in Hamilton and my family worked in the steel mills. The Ticats are Hamilton's team.

The summer after my sophomore year, I was lucky enough to secure an internship with the Hamilton Tiger-Cats. The internship extended to just over two years while I finished my degree thanks to the great mentors there who gave me a chance. The Tiger-Cats were fundamentally awful in terms of our production on the field and were not a very good football team unfortunately. During my time there, I believe our final record was

6-39. Historically, our winning percentage was one of the worst in the Canadian Football League. But the thing about the Tiger-Cats was that despite Hamilton's economic challenges, despite their own struggles and even a near-bankruptcy situation, they never faltered and they never closed.

In the Canadian Football League, the Labor Day games are the biggest deal other than the Grey Cup. Hamilton always hosts Toronto in the Labor Day Classic. It's the one day a year when Hamilton rises up against Toronto. The first professional sporting event I ever went to was a Labor Day Classic between the Ticats and the Toronto Argonauts with my dad. Fast forward, I was working for the Ticats and I was standing on the sideline of that game. That was the moment I decided sports would be part of my life and part of my career.

Working that game for my hometown team, I felt proud to be part of something that had meant so much to my family and the families in my city growing up. It made me realize what sports could do for a community. I saw people of different socioeconomic paths come together at dilapidated Ivor Wynne Stadium. It was a chance for all of them to wear black and yellow in solidarity, to chant and cheer and high-five each other when otherwise the rest of their day, the rest of their week, was a struggle. We weren't going to win - everybody knew we weren't going to win - but winning wasn't the reason why they showed up. It was about the chance to represent their city and where they were from and what they believed in.

The Ticats, for me, are proof that it's not about wins and losses; it's about community. The team had a struggling performance record on the field but an absolutely dominating performance off the field, to the point where it was one of the more respected franchises in the Canadian Football League. We were only winning an average of three out of 18 games a year, but we were packed to 97% capacity every night. When you can fill the stands to that level, that's a good day for any team. But for a team whose wins totaled single digits over 2½ years combined? That's really something special. We didn't sell wins and losses in Hamilton. Instead, we sold the chance to get out of the everyday and come to a game, to experience being part of something that meant so much to that community.

Working in sports, we have to understand that our job is to deal hope. We already have the love affair emotion side covered when it comes to marketing, so anybody can sell when you're winning. But if you can sell when you're losing, then you can make a difference for your team and your community.

A KICK IN THE GUT

• • • • • • •

BRAD SUTTON
Senior Associate Athletic Director for External Affairs
SMU

My parents are University of Kentucky alumni and die-hard fans, so Kentucky Basketball was one of the most important things in my life growing up. Even though we've won several National Championships, the moment that sticks with me the most is the pain I felt when we lost to Duke in the 1992 Elite Eight. The Kentucky team was coming off probation and their roster was mostly filled with honest-to-goodness spares. They weren't the most talented players, but they were guys with heart who played hard every time. It made us want to root for Kentucky even more.

I remember watching the game at home with my parents. Duke had won the National Championship the previous year and was heavily favored to win again. Nobody expected Kentucky to really challenge the Blue Devils that night. The game went into overtime and my mom left the room like she often does when games are tight. She was at the back of the house pacing nervously, unable to watch. My dad and I were in the living room glued to the screen, and I remember standing up during the last possession because I just couldn't stay seated. We were on the cusp of dethroning the reigning National Champions. We were leading by one point with only two seconds left on the clock when Duke threw the ball the length of the court to Christian Laettner and he hit a last-second jump shot to win the game, 104-103. I just fell to the floor, hoping they would wave it off as late. But they didn't, and Kentucky lost. I was crushed.

My dad is a more volatile sports watcher than I am, and I remember him throwing a pillow down on the couch and storming out of the room. I didn't envy him having to tell my mom what had happened, because I knew she wasn't going to take the news well either. That loss just ripped my heart out. To make things worse, it's one of those shots they inevitably show each year as part of the lead-in to March Madness games. To this day, whenever I see it I have this childlike hope that the ending will change somehow. And every single time, I still feel like somebody's kicking me in the gut.

Kentucky went on to win the National Championship a few years later in 1996, their first such victory since 1978. They had a really strong team that year and everyone expected them to win, so it was a great feeling but not as exciting as it would have been in 1992. I think when a win is unexpected, there's a different type of joy that makes it a little more special. Losing that game in 1992 after coming so close to an unexpected win taught me how to cope with one of the lowest lows of being a fan. That loss also taught me to enjoy the highs when they come and to never take winning for granted when it does happen.

⑤
CHAPTER FIVE
PEAKS OF ACHIEVEMENT

"The valleys of discouragement make more beautiful the peaks of achievement."
- Gordon Hinckley

I grew up during the Barry Switzer era of Oklahoma Football. We'd travel to Norman from Guthrie, OK and watch the Sooners lay victim to whoever dared enter Oklahoma Memorial Stadium. Winning wasn't just expected, it was a foregone conclusion. We never really entertained the idea that losing was a viable option. After Switzer left in the late eighties, the Sooners lost a step, but winning was still an expectation. We were no longer competing for a National Championship on an annual basis, but certain things were understood:

1. We'd have a winning record.
2. We'd be nationally-ranked.
3. We'd never get blown out.
4. We'd make a bowl game.
5. Under no circumstances would we ever lose to Oklahoma State.

1995

In 1995, two big things happened: One, I started my freshman year of college. Two, it was Howard Schnellenberger's first year as head coach at OU. The Sooners had made a change at the head coaching spot to restore glory to a waning football program and Schnelly was the answer. Or so we thought. The season didn't end up being the great turnaround we'd hoped for, but it was, after all, a rebuilding year. He needed time to right the ship. Our only losses toward the end of the season were to Top-10 teams, and we even managed to tie Texas in the Red River Rivalry.

Two games left: We'll beat Oklahoma State, as we had every year of my life since I'd been alive, lose to top-ranked Nebraska, take the off-season to lick our wounds and come back in '96 ready for a championship run.

Only that didn't happen. Remember chapter 4 of this book when I relayed my story of the most gut-wrenching loss I'd ever endured? Insert that story here in your mind because this is right when it happened. At the time, I was hopeful that this was going to be an isolated incident. A blemish on the otherwise spotless Oklahoma Football program. What I soon realized was that this was the beginning of a long road back to glory.

That ended up being Schnellenberger's only year at Oklahoma. He was promptly fired after the season and, while I'm sure there were plenty of reasons for his forced resignation, I like to believe that he was let go because he lost to OSU and caused me so much personal anguish.

Unfortunately, his replacement, John Blake, didn't fare much better. Three losing seasons in a row and my entire college years were spent watching my beloved Sooners get embarrassed week after week after week. I attended nearly every home football game during college. My friends and I joked about how long it would take our Sooners to commit a false-start penalty and the "unders" usually won. It was a comedy of errors, only I saw little comedy in it. This football program was the entire reason I wanted to go to OU. I dreamed of coming to OU and seeing my Sooners win a National Championship while I was a student. Not only were they not living up to that expectation, they couldn't even manage a winning season.

To say that this was the deepest valley in the history of the Oklahoma Football program would be an understatement.

It. Was. Awful.

My 1995 must have been a lot like Leon Costello's 1984. Leon is the Director of Athletics at Montana State University and when we spoke, he talked a lot about the heartbreak of growing up a Chicago Cubs fan. The biggest difference is that he didn't have the years of seeing the Cubs win championships. No, as a Cubs fan there were no peaks. Just valleys. Which is why in 1984 when they were playing for the National League pennant, Leon's hopes were high that he'd finally get to witness a championship and a trip to the World Series.

The Cubs had a two-game lead on the Padres that year in the NLCS but went on to lose three straight, keeping the curse alive. It was gut-wrenching for Leon and every other Cubs fan out there. They were ascending to the peak and had it in their grasp, only to have the rug pulled out from under them. *Again.*

But the worst, *the absolute worst*, was the Bartman game.

In 2003, the Cubs were 5 outs away from the World Series when Moisés Alou attempted to catch a foul ball off the bat of Marlins' second baseman Luis Castillo. Cubs fan, Steve Bartman, reached for the ball from his front row seat, deflected it and disrupted a potential catch by Alou. The Cubs ended up surrendering eight runs that inning and losing the game, 8–3. When they were eliminated in the seventh game the next day, the incident was seen as the "first domino" in the turning point of the series.

The Deeper the Valley, the Higher the Peak

Fortunately for me, it took me an extra semester to graduate. Why is that fortunate? Because Bob Stoops was hired after the 1998 season and in 1999 (my second senior year), he launched the Sooners on an ascent that would take the Sooners to the highest peak the program had seen in years. And thanks to my inability to finish school in four years, I can say that I attended school during the Stoops era.

In 2000, OU fans were riding high after a 7-5 season and a trip to the Independence Bowl, but no one could have expected what was to come.

The Sooners started the season strong, going 4-0 against opponents that a couple years before would have given them trouble. They rolled into Dallas for the first big test of the season: Oklahoma vs. Texas. I was scared to death of that game, but it ended up being one of the most euphoric sports experiences of my life. OU dismantled Texas in a 63-14 rout on a cold, rainy Saturday at the Cotton Bowl.

OU beat the #5, #2 and #1 teams in the country in a single month, taking the number one ranking for the first time since my childhood and sending OU fans into a frenzy. Norman was as exciting a place to be as any town in the country. And then, by some miracle, OU went on to beat Florida State in the National Championship game. OU shocked the world that year and returned Sooner Football to glory.

Words can't describe what that football season did for OU fans and the state of Oklahoma. As I'm sure words can't describe what winning the

World Series last year did for Cubs fans and the city of Chicago.

Leon Costello was in Chicago for Game 5 of the World Series and told me it was one of the greatest experiences of his life. One comment he makes in his story has stuck with me since we spoke "Cubs fans finally got to witness a World Series victory in Wrigley Field. Nobody wanted to leave."

Victory does that for us, doesn't it? It makes us want to live in that moment forever. Cubs fans stayed at Wrigley field for a good half-hour after Game 5. They had reached a peak and a few days later, they'd reach the ultimate peak, winning the World Series for the first time in 108 years. All those years of suffering made the victory that much sweeter.

No one likes to lose. No one likes to spend a day in the valley, much less 108 years. Spending my college years as the basement dwellers of college football made the 2000 season far more magical than any sports experience I've ever had. So when the design job came open at OU Athletics, I couldn't imagine not taking that opportunity. My career path might have been entirely different had it not been for that 2000 OU football season.

Winning in sports lifts people up and brings them together in a way that few things can. It takes perfect strangers and creates pockets in time when they become best friends. It unites communities, forms bonds between family and friends, and creates memories that last a lifetime.

The stories in Chapter 5 are about winning. But the great thing about them is they're all about unexpected wins or big wins after long droughts of losing. When you expect it, another win is just that: another win. But when your team has been through the valleys of discouragement or it looks like all is lost, their peaks of achievement are that much greater. Winning just isn't as fun when you don't know how it feels to lose.

MY MEMORABLE AUBURN MOMENT

• • • • • • •

SCOTT STRICKLIN
Director of Athletics
University of Florida

While working at Auburn early in my career, I remember one baseball game that defined my five years there.

We were playing in the NCAA Regional at Florida State for the opportunity to go to the College World Series. During the first game of the tournament, our All-SEC catcher got hit by a pitch and broke his wrist. It was, literally, a bad break.

Our backup catcher was a kid from Tallahassee. His name was David Ross. David's strength was his defense and we were certainly going to miss our starting catcher's bat in the lineup. However, the whole team pulled together that day, played hard and managed to stay alive. Two days later, we had yet to lose in the tournament and went up against host FSU in the winner's bracket. We knew winning the game would put us in the driver's seat. Heading into the ninth inning, we were down 7-3. We managed to score a couple runs to make it 7-5, then got two runners on base with two outs and David Ross coming to the plate.

David was so nervous that it seemed his knees were practically knocking when he stepped into the batter's box. We were playing in his hometown and he was 0-for-4 for the game. It was make-or-break for our team and it all rested on his shoulders. David got two strikes on him and it seemed like he would soon be the final out.

Next pitch — swing and a miss.

FSU's players poured onto the field and the crowd went wild.

But then we noticed the umpire was waving his hands. *FOUL BALL!* The catcher had not held on to the tip. The game wasn't over.

So the FSU players returned to the dugout, our guys went back to their bases and David and the pitcher had to square off again. The next pitch perfectly painted the corner and looked like strike three. We were shocked it wasn't and the pitcher seemed furious. Now, David should have struck out twice, but he's still up there trying to find a way to get on base.

The pitcher then hung a slider and David absolutely crushed the ball. I remember watching it soar over the wall, a good 400-some feet, for a grand slam to win the game 8-7 on a walk-off. In a split second, we went from agony to ecstasy. Our fans went wild, hugging everybody whether they knew them or not. It was incredible. It was one of the more remarkable things I've been a part of in college athletics.

David went on to experience some other memorable moments. Yes, that David Ross was the one who won a World Series in both Boston and last fall, at age 39, became the oldest player to hit a home run in a World Series when he did it in Game 7 for the Chicago Cubs in what turned out to be the final game of his professional career. Not a bad way to go out.

But his big fly for Auburn is still one of the most famous home runs in school history and I'm sure it's still one of the coolest memories of David's athletic career. Nobody could have predicted that win. It was unbelievable. When there's so much tension and your team ends up winning, the release of emotion is just so powerful.

Those moments don't happen very often. When they do, they're special.

MORE THAN JUST A GAME

• • • • • • •

LEON COSTELLO
Director of Athletics
Montana State University

I'm a huge Cubs fan. I grew up in Iowa where most people were either Cubs, Cardinals or Twins fans. I think part of the reason I chose the Cubs was because their games were played during the day (they didn't have lights for their field at the time) so I could get home from school and watch a Cubs game before my parents got home from work.

I remember when the Cubs played the Padres in the 1984 National League Championship Series. The Cubs had a two-game lead but then lost the next three games. At the time, I was too young to understand the significance of it or understand the history of the Cubs. I just knew that my team had lost and I was really disappointed they weren't going to the World Series.

It happened again in 2003 with the Marlins: another Cubs World Series dream crushed by a three-game losing streak. In the sixth game of the National League Championship that year, the Cubs were leading the series 3-2 and were up 3-0 with only five outs standing between them and the World Series. We were so close! Then the Steve Bartman incident happened. He was the Cubs fan who reached for a foul ball and disrupted a potential catch by Cubs out-fielder Moises Alou. Everybody looked at the Bartman incident as another epi-sode of the curse striking again but he wasn't the only reason the Cubs lost that game or the one after it. I think he just became the focal point for everyone's frustration over the Cubs getting so close to going to the World Series and once again not being able to get it done.

In 2015, the Cubs made it back to the National League Championship Series only to get swept by the New York Mets. Being on the cusp so many times only to have your heart broken over and over is hard on fans. You get to the point where you're like, *Okay, it's just one of those things.* But at the same time you're thinking, *Is this whole thing just going to go on forever? Aren't we ever going to make it?* It's excruciating to care about a team so much and want something to happen so badly.

When the Cubs finally made it into the World Series in 2016, it was like it was meant to be. There were so many parallels to the drought that it was scary. There are 108 stitches in a baseball and it had been 108 years since the Cubs had won a World Series. There are several other coincidences between the Cubs and the number 108, including the length of two movies that show them winning the World Series and the distance from home plate to the right and left field corners of Wrigley Field. When I read about it, I looked at my wife in amazement and said, *We just got the job at Montana State and moved here and our street address is 108. What are the odds? 108 is a lucky number, it's meant to be!*

The night before the World Series started I was given an opportunity to purchase a ticket to Game 5 at Wrigley Field. There was only one ticket available so I wouldn't be able to take my wife or my brother, who's also a lifelong Cubs fan. After spending several hours looking at flights and hotels and not finding anything, I told my wife, *It's just not going to work.* She looked me in the eye and said, *You've been a Cubs fan your whole life and for as long as I've known you, you've told me that if they made it to the World Series you were going to go. You're going. If you don't, you'll regret it for the rest of your life. Now I'm going to get ready for bed and by the time I'm done I want you to have purchased your ticket and your hotel.* I ended up booking a hotel that was all the way out by O'Hare airport. Thank goodness for Uber.

Game 5 was on Sunday so I flew into Chicago on Saturday. I was also a Bulls fan growing up and the Bulls were playing on Saturday night. I reached out to Greg McDermott, who was the Head Basketball Coach when I worked at the University of Northern Iowa. Greg's son Doug plays for the Chicago Bulls. I asked Greg, *Is there any way Doug can get me tickets to the Bulls game?* Greg told me, *I'm not going to be there, just use my ticket.* It was a great way to start a great sports weekend. Watching the Bulls with my friend's son on the team while the World Series was going on right there in Chicago was an incredible experience. The next day I went to Wrigley Field about four hours before game time so I could walk around the stadium and buy souvenirs for my family. I remember seeing the marquis at the front of the stadium, *Cubs vs. Indians, World Series, Game 5,* and taking a picture. It was one of those pinch-me moments: *the Cubs were actually in the World Series and I was actually there to see it!* It was something I had dreamed about since I was a kid. Before the game I remember thinking, *I'm going to get a program just in case they go on a run here and win the World Series.* I bought a program and didn't even open it other than to put my ticket stub inside and put it in my backpack.

Being in the stadium for that game was amazing. I have been to many but this one was obviously different. It's not like watching the game on TV where the cameras are so focused on the strike zone. When you're there in person you're able to look around, watch the players warming up, see reactions from fans, and just take everything in. The Indians had a 3-1 series lead coming into Game 5 and when they scored the first run I was like, *Oh no, here we go again.* But when Chris Bryant hit the home run the tide had turned. The Cubs eventually won Game 5, the first World Series win at Wrigley Field since 1945. The energy and the noise in Wrigley Field was one of the most intense things I've ever experienced. At the end of the game, the traditional singing of *Go Cubs Go* is something I will never forget. Afterward, nobody left the stadium for quite a while. I think the Cubs fans just wanted that moment to last forever, to relish finally being in the World Series and winning such an important game at home.

A few nights after the Cubs had clinched their World Series victory with a three game winning streak, I was putting my four year old son to bed. Out of the blue, he looked up at me and said, *Dad, the Cubs always win.* As somebody who has cheered for the Cubs for so long and seen them go through some not-so-good years over the past four decades, it's the last thing I would have said. I had to chuckle because that put everything in perspective: in his young life as a fan, that's the only thing he knows.

For a lot of people who are Cubs fans, that win changed their outlook on life. I know many people think, *Come on, it's just a game.* But it's so much more than that to so many people. For fans who have invested so much of themselves in supporting a team, a win like that can create a sense of happiness and well-being that will stay with them forever. Just like it's more than a game for our student-athletes who learn indelible life lessons from their coaches, their teammates and their opponents. If it were just a game, the saying, *The thrill of victory and the agony of defeat,* wouldn't ring so true. The depth of emotion sports evokes and the impact it can have on somebody's life is what makes sports so powerful and so much more than just a game.

BROTHERHOOD
& REDEMPTION

• • • • • • •

RYAN PECK

*Executive Senior Associate Athletic Director
for External Affairs*
University of North Texas

When I was growing up, playing sports was the most important thing in the world to me. So when it came time to choose a college, my decision was 100% based on finding the best soccer program that would take me. For a guy who wasn't quite tall enough, fast enough or good enough to compete at the highest levels, that meant keeping an open mind about where I might go to school.

There was a Division II school called Lander University a little way from where I grew up. It's a small school about 2½ hours from Atlanta. Lander's soccer program had a strong winning tradition, a well-respected coach in Van Taylor and they wanted me on their team, so that's where I decided to go.

Playing soccer at Lander was amazing and epitomized the student-athlete experience for me. My senior year, we ended up being ranked in the Top 10 nationally and hosted the conference tournament at our campus. It seemed like everything was lining up in our favor for a long postseason run, and I was excited to see how far we could make it. For me and my fellow seniors, being ranked so highly and seeing the possibility of a championship ahead was just an incredible way to experience the end of our college playing careers.

In the first round of the Peach Belt Conference tournament, we played

North Georgia. We had a better record, we were on our home turf and we were favored to win. We were feeling confident and were already thinking about the other games ahead of us, so it was a complete shock when we ended up losing in overtime. I couldn't believe that we had gotten upset in the first round! I was shattered, and so were my fellow seniors. None of us could believe that our season and our college soccer careers had ended that way. We all knew that professional soccer wasn't in the cards for us, but we didn't want it to end and felt we deserved a couple more college games. Suddenly it was all over, ended by a game we should have won. To finish our season like that, especially when our hopes had been so high, was devastating. Without soccer, we did not know what to do or what was next.

While we were mourning our loss, Coach Taylor got an unexpected phone call. As fate would have it, we received an at-large bid to keep playing. We were headed to the NCAA Soccer Tournament and couldn't believe what we were hearing. *Could it really be true?* We were getting another chance!

As word spread amongst our teammates, we made our way to campus. We were overwhelmed with joy and excitement and a sense of disbelief. For the seniors on the team, it was a particularly emotional moment: getting a second chance at our soccer careers was something we hadn't thought possible. I remember standing right there in the quad at Lander University, singing and doing soccer chants with my teammates. It was unscripted and euphoric. You could hear our excited shouts all the way across campus: *Let's all go to nationals! Let's all go to nationals! Nana-na-naa! Nana-na-naa!* and *Ooo-L-A-N, Oh-L-A-N, Oh-D-E-R! We are the boys, the boys of Lander! Oh-L-A-N, Oh-D-E-R! HEY!!!*

Now with a new opportunity in the NCAA tournament, we pulled out the first round win in penalty kicks over #19 UNC Pembroke. Our second game happened to be against our rival, #8 ranked Clayton State. They were the best team in our conference that year. We were going back and forth, back and forth, matching each other play for play and scoring chance for scoring chance. Chiddy, a fellow senior from Nigeria, was a super lightning-fast forward, able to beat anybody using his speed, but he wasn't always the best at scoring goals. So Chiddy takes a big touch just beyond midfield, goes around a defender, and he's getting ready to shoot from about 35 yards out and we're like, *No, don't do it!* But Chiddy goes for it anyway. He rips the shot perfectly and the ball goes into the top right corner, an unsaveable shot. We battle, we hold on, we pull the upset victory over Clayton State on their home field. We won and couldn't believe it! In that moment, everything around me stopped and nothing else mattered. It was just our team, our victory, our celebration. It was pure bliss.

The win over Clayton State got us an NCAA Southeast Region Championship ring, which is still one of my most prized possessions. Every year, I wear that ring for one day on November 13. It's the day we won that game - which also happens to be Chiddy's birthday. It's a small annual reminder of that moment and my teammates.

That triumph is still special to all 30 of the guys who were on that team, and many of us stay in touch. The extraordinary bond amongst teammates is hard to explain. We had guys from Columbia, Nigeria, England, Finland, Bolivia, and from all over the country. For whatever reason, we were brought together to be part of this Division II soccer program in Greenwood, South Carolina, that created relationships and friends for life. For me, the greatest moment didn't involve 100,000 people in the stands on a football Saturday. It was simply that moment of brotherhood and redemption on the soccer field.

A WATERSHED MOMENT

• • • • • • •

AYO TAYLOR-DIXON
Senior Associate Athletics Director
Georgia Tech

When I began working at the University of South Florida in October 2006, their football program was still young and was actually celebrating its 10th season. USF had only been part of the Big East Conference for a year when I got there and part of the reason I wanted to work there was because of the great opportunity to be a part of many firsts. That type of opportunity doesn't happen very often in college athletics.

I remember being in the middle of some serious planning for the 2007 football season when our new Executive Associate AD, Bill McGillis, called a meeting with our entire external staff. Bill looked around the room and asked, *Who thinks we can sell out a game?* I raised my hand, but not very many other people did. At that time, the highest attendance we had ever had was 49,212 at the very first game vs. Kentucky Wesleyan. The capacity of Raymond James Stadium, where we played, was 65,786 and many people on the staff were skeptical that we would ever reach that number.

We started our season off with a win at home, then went to Auburn and beat them in a dramatic overtime game. It was our biggest victory to date and people started to really get excited! We had a bye week following that game, which was great because it gave us some time to make additional plans for our upcoming games as our demand increased and to let the buzz build. We defeated North Carolina in front of a home crowd of nearly 40,000 the week after the bye week and the hot market was a snowball building massive momentum. We already had a number of things already planned for our game against West Virginia the following week because it was a marquis game on our schedule. We had planned a student concert and a big youth football day, and were working on another group sales effort. Having all those things already lined up for the West Virginia game that was on a Friday night must have been fate, because it was perfect timing combined with the success we were having on the field. When we were ranked for the first time and beat North Carolina, it added fuel to the fire for our fans and we sold out for the West Virginia game.

I vividly remember all the planning that went into that game because we were facing challenges we had never faced before. From having to navigate the additional challenges a sold out game presented to working with the Tampa Stadium Authority and dealing with traffic, managing credential and parking requests and needing increased media parking and dealing with the Fire Marshall to approve our post game fireworks show, there were just a few things going on that week! It was also the first time we had ever done a student concert in the stadium or planned post-game fireworks so there were many moving parts. I do not think I got any sleep at all that week. On Tuesday, we had our weekly game ops meeting at the TSA where Bill McGillis and I showed the group a video of a game between two other schools where the home team upset their opponent and all the students rushed the field. We said, *We are not going to encourage our students to rush the field but if they do, we need to be prepared for how quickly something like this could happen.*

The USF student body really got behind that game. Ticket demand was so high that we had to have a student campout outside our basketball arena, the USF Sun Dome, for tickets the Sunday night before the game. We probably had about 3,000 students sleeping out there that night and it was just organized chaos. I did not get any sleep. I just kept going back and forth between my office and the campout to make sure there were not any incidents. It turned out fine because the kids were all just really excited and happy to be there. You should have seen the line the next day to get student tickets as it wrapped all the way around the Sun Dome!

We sold out the game. Our fans and student turnout was amazing. We were ranked No. 18 heading into that game and West Virginia was ranked No. 5, and the game ended up being the most watched game between two ranked teams on a Friday night on ESPN at that time. It was an exciting game and our players worked hard to prove they deserved the national spotlight. I spent the entire third quarter meeting with the police and Stadium Operations to talk about how we could handle all the different scenarios that could happen at the end of the game. *Hey, if this happens what are we going to do? How are we going to handle it? How are we going to get the teams off? How are we going to make sure we do not have any incidents?* It was nerve-wracking but exciting all at the same time.

As the game ended, I remember standing on the field, looking at the score and realizing we were going to win. We beat West Virginia 21-13 in front of our first-ever sold out crowd. Everything we had planned and worked so hard for had produced a tremendous accomplishment for our university, and I just felt this immense sense of satisfaction that we had been able to do it.

That win against West Virginia is something I will never forget. It was a watershed moment for our program and gained us national attention. Looking back on all the effort that went into that season and achieving our goal of filling the stadium makes me proud. It was a truly remarkable moment.

THE GAME THAT MATTERED MOST

• • • • • • •

STEPHANIE REMPE
Deputy Athletic Director
Texas A&M University

Everyone in my family – my parents, brother, uncle and cousins – went to the University of Arizona. The rivalry of the UA vs. ASU game in any sport was intense and that intensity was particularly strong in our family. I grew up passionately despising Arizona State. My dad, still to this day, speaks with venom regarding anything ASU. My mom, on the other hand, is fairly easygoing. However, one of my most vivid childhood memories is going to Coffin Corner of the ASU Stadium and watching my parents lose a bit of their composure cheering against ASU. I even remember my mom tearing the bottom out of her cup so that when the ASU fans chanted *ASU! ASU!* she could use it like a megaphone to yell *Sucks!* She would never have done something like that in any other situation! But when Arizona was playing ASU in any sport, the gloves came off. That rivalry is something everyone in my family takes pretty seriously.

Continuing family tradition, after some agonizing debates, I chose to go to Arizona. I was a three sport athlete throughout high school and after one semester in college I knew I needed some more structure in my life. Sports had always provided that structure and without it I was a bit lost. As a result, I reached out to the UA volleyball coach that spring. At the time, the coach had never accepted a walk on before. The walk on process was long and drawn out: I kept going to every practice and trying to prove myself at every opportunity until finally, after several agonizing weeks of not knowing which way it would go, I made the team!

During my first three years there, we lost to ASU every single time we played them. It didn't seem to matter how well we were playing otherwise, we just couldn't win those rivalry games. I took those losses really personally; each time, it was like I was letting my family down. I vowed that we would beat ASU my senior year no matter what it took, and I invested a lot of emotional energy in motivating our team to do so. We played ASU twice during the regular season that year and both times we thought we had a chance to break the streak, but we ended up losing both matches after five games. That was difficult for our entire team, but I think I took it the hardest of anyone. I couldn't believe that we had gone 0-8 against ASU during my career as a Wildcat.

Despite those two losses to ASU, we had our best-ever conference finish my senior year and placed fourth in the PAC-10. Beating No. 1 UCLA at home on senior night and beating No. 2 Stanford made it an incredible season. It was a huge moment for Arizona Women's Volleyball! Next was the NCAA tournament and I still remember the selection show. First up was Lamar at home and if we beat Lamar we would have to play at ASU in the second round – I could not believe it! I didn't want ASU to take away our opportunity to go to the Sweet Sixteen and I didn't want to end my college playing career with another loss to our archrivals! It really got to me, to the point where it started to affect everything I did. After a couple of practices, Coach Dave Rubio pulled me aside and said, *Stephanie, this is not acceptable. You can't act like this. You've got to choose what you're going to focus on and whether or not you're on board.* He was right, of course. The only way being angry at ASU was going to do me any good was if I refocused my energy on the game itself.

When we went to ASU for the second round game, it was do or die time. We put everything we had into it! With the longstanding rivalry between the two schools and a trip to the Sweet 16 on the line, you can only imagine how intense things were on the court. The match went five games but Arizona was finally vindicated: we won! The end of that final game is a moment I'll never forget. I'm honestly not sure what made me happier: the excitement of making it into the Sweet 16 or simply the satisfaction of finally beating our biggest rival. After all the years I had spent cheering against ASU and all the energy I had invested in trying to beat them during the past four years, it was an unbelievable feeling. We might have been 1-8 against ASU during my career, but the one game we had beaten them in was the game that mattered the most.

A POWERFUL THING

• • • • • • •

CHRIS BAIN
Assistant Athletic Director for Marketing
University of Pittsburgh

While I've been fortunate to go to a lot of sporting events and high pro-file games, the most powerful moment I've experienced wasn't something like seeing Derek Jeter hit his 3,000th hit. It was simply realizing just how incredible winning can be when you don't take it for granted.

One of my good friends is a guy I had worked with at the University of Central Florida. He was a huge Pittsburgh Pirates fan, and I always used to make fun of him for that. The Pirates were just so bad! They were always trying to trade for Yankees cast-offs, guys who were a little bit washed up, and hoping that things would work out better for them. It seemed like it never did and their fans always struggled with disappointment.

I moved to Pittsburgh in 2013, and that year the Pirates made the Wildcard game. It was unprecedented. The Pirates hadn't played a postsea-son game since 1992. As a true sports town, Pittsburgh went berserk. So of course, my buddy Brad reached out to me and said, *Hey, I'm coming up! I've got to be there for this game. Let's get tickets, let's go!* With so much hype and excitement about the game, ticket prices skyrocketed quickly. We didn't want to spend a ton of money so we bought standing room only tickets. For us, it was really just about getting into PNC Park and being there in person to experience everything firsthand.

The day of the game was like nothing I'd ever seen before. The city of

Pittsburgh practically shut down. Everyone's focus was on the Pirates and you could just feel the excitement building as game time drew nearer. People started block parties at 2 o'clock in the afternoon for the 7 o'clock game. Everyone here at the athletic department left early. It didn't matter who you were or whether you had a history with the team, the opportunity to be part of the moment was too good to miss out on.

PNC Park is a beautiful ballpark and if you have certain seats, you get a fantastic view of the city in the background. I'd been to one Pirate's game before this and it was a great atmosphere. But the day of the Wildcard Game, PNC Park surpassed itself. The place was sold out and the atmosphere was simply unbelievable. They gave out black towels for fans to create a blackout and the roar of the crowd was almost unbearably loud. The Pirates were up against the Cincinnati Reds, who had made it into the playoffs for the third time in four years. The Pirates took the lead in the second inning and never looked back, winning the game 6-2.

The euphoria and feeling of vindication in the stadium was overwhelming. I'll never forget looking around and seeing grown men weeping and hugging each other. There were guys who were there with their dads, their brothers, their friends and they were all just completely overcome by emotion. There were young men who had spent their entire lives hoping for this moment, who hadn't even been alive the last time the Pirates made it to the postseason. And you could sense this incredible release from the pain and agony these fans had gone through over the past two decades. All the misery that goes with faithfully supporting a losing team for so long just magnified the joy they had in winning that Wildcard game.

I might not be a Pirates fan, but I remember growing up and playing ball in the front yard with my dad, pretending that the Yankees won the pennant and things like that. That day at PNC Park, I got to see father-and-son duos who did those same things, had those same hopes, and finally saw their dreams come to fruition. With the Yankees, you almost took winning for granted because it happened so much. But these guys had been down for so long and had been disappointed so often that winning meant a lot more to them. It was a powerful thing to witness.

SUN DEVILS

• • • • • • •

BRIAN WHITE
Executive Associate Athletic Director, External Relations
University of Missouri

Both of my parents started their careers as high school teachers and coaches, so I grew up around athletics. My dad was an athletic director my entire life, and we had the opportunity to live in several different states as his career progressed from school to school. For us, sports was family. All of my uncles weren't really my blood uncles, they were coaches or administrators who worked with my dad. Student-athletes spent time at our house and we spent time at their practices and games. My dad went to everything and he'd always take us with him. I loved it.

When I was in 7th grade, my dad accepted a position with Arizona State and we moved to Tempe, Arizona. I immediately became a full-fledged fan of the Sun Devils. After the games, I would work in the equipment room cleaning up the gear and uniforms. We'd take the jerseys, separate them from the pads, and put the jerseys in the laundry. Those jerseys were completely soaked with sweat, almost as if somebody had thrown them in a pool. It was a sweaty and disgusting job but I didn't care. We got to eat fried chicken with the players if we cleaned up their equipment and that was good enough for me.

That was 1996, the year of the Jake Plummer/Pat Tillman Rose Bowl run. Pat Tillman was a real character and even then you knew how great a leader he was. His personality just took over that team, and it was really cool to see. We were supposed to be pretty good that year, but the team blew all predictions out of the water and ended up undefeated. It was a magical year but gut-wrenching at the same time, because we had so many close finishes. Feeling the near-agony of suspense followed by the thrill of winning was the most fun I've ever had being part of a team. I remember being at the game when the Sun Devils played Nebraska, and Nebraska was the number one team in the country at the time. They were the two-time defending National Champions and were on a 26 game winning streak, so everyone thought we were going to get killed. But our team played aggressively and pulled off a huge upset, winning the game 19 to nothing! It was a shocking win and the stands erupted in celebration. Nobody had shut out Nebraska since before I was even born! Everyone stormed the field, cheering and yelling as they tore the goal post down and carried it out of the stadium. I remember trying to run out onto the field but Tom Collins, who was one of my dad's Associate Athletic Directors, thought better of it and held me in the corner and said, *No, you're not going on the goal post!* It was a prime example of a time when my dad's colleagues were more like family than co-workers.

The experiences I had that year made me think for the first time, *Wow, I really, really want to find a way to work in sports.* Even though we lived other places after that, Arizona State had a special place in my heart, and I returned to Arizona State as a full-time marketing intern after I graduated from Notre Dame.

As a marketing intern, one of my jobs was to help clear the field after games. When you're working at that level, you're kind of a jack-of-all-trades and extra manpower for whatever needs to get done. This particular day, as the rest of the fans were leaving a guy came up to me and said, *Hey, can I just get on the field? I just want to take a picture because my dad is dying and I told him I'd take a picture on the field.* He must have seen that I had a credential and thought I had some kind of authority. I wasn't sure what I could do because I had zero power, but I felt badly for his situation. I looked over at my boss and she kind of waves me on and says, *Yeah, go ahead.*

I walked the guy onto the field and out to the 50-yard line. He gave me his phone to take the picture, so I backed up to get a good shot for his dad who was dying. But the next thing I know, this guy pulls out a little container and pours something onto the field! I didn't understand what was happening. The guy looked at me and said, *My dad always wanted to be buried with his ashes on this field. I'm sorry I lied to you but that was the only way I felt I could do it.* I was stunned. I don't know anything else about that guy or his dad, because he disappeared pretty quickly after that. But I've always thought of that moment as a testament to the passion of sports and how powerfully people identify with being a fan.

SOMETHING TO BELIEVE IN

• • • • • • •

JOSEPH R. CASTIGLIONE
Vice President and Director of Athletics
University of Oklahoma

I have witnessed some of the most amazing achievements by student-athletes that one could ever witness. Among those, there's one that really cemented for me the notion of how important sports can be in people's lives.

The '90s, not quite a throw-back to the dust bowl days, were still really difficult for the University of Oklahoma and its fan base. When I started working here in 1998, there were a number of systemic issues and the athletics department was struggling financially. Even though we had some successes like the basketball team making the NCAA tournament that year, morale was low both internally and externally. The sport that drives so much of the passion and finances for the university as a whole is football, and in the '90s football wasn't going well for OU.

Football transcends sports at Oklahoma. It goes beyond the excitement of winning games to impact people's psyches. People say that when Oklahoma's winning, the air smells cleaner and the sun is brighter. The history of the program dates back to 1895, before Oklahoma achieved statehood, and is intertwined with the history of the state and its families. When you talk about the Sooners, you're talking about football that spans generations. Our fans identify with us because of what they did as a child with their parents and the traditions they continued with their own children and handed down to their grandchildren. It's one of those things you can't fully appreciate until you've experienced it first-hand.

That brings us back to 2000, the end of an uncharacteristic football drought and renewed pride. When we hired Bob Stoops, the pendulum began swinging back in the right direction. In his first season, 1999, we went 7-5 and played in a bowl game. Then in his second year, we were undefeated and won perhaps the most improbable of OU's seven National Championships. It caused a seismic change among our people.

As we traveled throughout the state the following spring, I can't tell you how many people came up to us to talk about what that championship meant to them. It happened everywhere we went within the state and anywhere else we had large concentrations of alums like the Dallas/Ft. Worth metroplex, Houston and even Wichita. Many were emotional in describing how they had thought the great championship years were over only to have them return in stunning fashion. I don't just mean, *Hey, I'm so excited, thanks Coach, this is a great year!* It was like they were baring their souls to us about what that National Championship meant, their memories of going to games over generations, and how important a day or a weekend trip had been because in many cases their vacations were centered around those games. As much as they loved the Sooners, it was more about the connection our team had with one of their most cherished life experiences.

There's a lot of excitement and celebration and fun that comes with winning a championship, but for our fans it meant so much more. It has been said many times that sports mimic life: the ups and downs, the difficult periods where you feel like you might never reach your goals, the satisfaction of succeeding. I think that season showed me the truth in the axiom. Seeing Oklahoma achieve greatness on a national level, seeing people respect the state and university and the student-athletes that helped get the team to that level, meant everything to our fans. The success of the football team, in a way, gave them a feeling of personal achievement too because they kind of lived vicariously through that team. Whatever it was they were facing – a sickness; a tragedy in their family; losing a job; being alone – that team gave them something to believe in. It gave them an escape and a getaway, but more than that it helped them believe in themselves and overcome whatever was going on in their lives. It was the feeling that you could win, you could achieve, you could overcome all the naysayers and make it to the top. When I think about why we do what we do, my mind always goes back to that 2000 football season. I feel blessed that we have the opportunity to impact people's lives that way.

6
CHAPTER SIX
NO SHAVING ON GAMEDAYS

❝ It's bad luck to be superstitious. ❞
- Andrew W. Mathis

One of the most fascinating things to me is the extent to which we will go to help create wins. Obviously, we build huge stadiums and the fanciest facilities to lure the best athletes. We spend millions of dollars to hire the best coaches. We scream at the top of our lungs to create a hostile environment for opponents. All of these things are rational. It makes sense to do these things in support of our favorite teams. So what about the irrational things we do? What about the crazy, superstitious things we do that make absolutely no sense, yet we do them anyway?

I can't say for certain, but I truly don't think I've ever shaved on the day of a Sooner football game. It must have started back in college when I rarely shaved at all and certainly wasn't going to go through the trouble on a Saturday before a football game. Then, when I started my career and had to shave on a regular basis, I took Saturdays off and justified it with a superstitious rule: *No Shaving on Gamedays!*

It just so happens that the year I started my professional career was also the same year OU won its first football National Championship since 1985. And without a doubt, my not shaving on gamedays was a big factor in that championship. Sure, we had the Heisman runner-up in the QB position. We had Roy Williams, one of the best defensive backs in history, anchoring our backfield. And they deserve some credit, I guess. But let's be honest.

A lot of their success was due to my not shaving on the days they had to compete.

I am not a superstitious person. I'll walk under a ladder, scoff at breaking a mirror and will even invite a black cat to cross my path. I think superstition is downright silly. But when it comes to sports, I'll embrace anything that might help my team to victory. If we seem to be doing better when I watch from the kitchen, I stay in the kitchen. If we score when I leave the room, I will try that again when we need another score. Hat on backwards, sideways or on the floor... sitting on the couch, the ottoman or standing up... cheering your team to victory includes finding that balance of exactly what one must do to please the gods of sports so they will bless your team with a win.

Believe it or not, Old Hat was even named after a sports superstition. My freshman year of college in 1995, I purchased a brand new OU ball cap. From that point on, I wore that hat to every OU home game I attended from then until we lost to Oklahoma State in 2001. I took that hat off that day (the luck had run out of it) and never wore it to a game again. In fact, I wouldn't put it back on my head until we beat Oklahoma State again, and then I retired it for good.

That hat sat on a shelf in my home office for years. It was tattered and torn, dirty and faded. So when I was trying to come up with a name for the company I was starting, it made sense to call it Old Hat. It seems like a lot of sports fans have that "old hat" they wear to all the games. And thus, out of superstition was born the name of the company that has defined my career.

In the Fabric of Sports

Superstition is an integral part of sports. Most of us know it doesn't affect the outcome of the game, but it just makes it more fun. I also think it gives fans the ability to feel like they're actually a part of the team. As fans, we want to participate in the game. We can't be the ones hitting the home runs or diving to block a penalty kick. So we do other things to feel like we have a role in helping our team win. It's crazy. It's illogical. But we do it.

Matt Roberts, Director of Athletics at the College of Charleston, says, *Superstition is in the fabric of sports. It's just a part of it. And even though it's proven over a long time that what you wear, what you eat, the routines and everything that you do on the day of a game or day before the game have been as much ineffective as they have been effective, I still do it.*

And it's not just Matt. The question of superstition was something we included in our fan survey. We asked fans if, when it comes to sporting events, they consider themselves superstitious. Forty-four percent of respondents said that yes, in fact, they are. In a second survey of more passionate fans, we found that 62% of them were superstitious when it comes to sports. So I think it's safe to assume that somewhere between those two numbers is pretty accurate. Which means that roughly half of the people at any given sporting event are doing something a bit superstitious to ensure their team will win.

The best part is we asked these fans *why* they do these superstitious things. We wanted to know if they thought it could actually affect the outcome of the game, if they did it for fun or if it was something that was a part of their DNA and they just couldn't help it. We found that 20% of superstitious fans actually believe (or want to believe) that it can affect the outcome. I love this statistic because it shows the level of irrationality that exists in sports fans.

For me, not shaving on gamedays is just a part of the experience and makes it more fun. I don't believe it's going to change anything about how the team performs, but it's one more gameday tradition I have that adds to the excitement of the day. Thirty percent of people surveyed perform their superstitious acts for the same reason. They feel like it makes the experience more fun. Another 30% do it because they say they just can't help it. I know what they mean. As much as it defies logic and rationality, there are times I find myself doing absurd things like watching the game from my bedroom instead of the living room in order to change their luck. I just can't help it!

We asked fans to share with us some of their craziest superstitions. Here are some of my favorites:

> When my team kicks a field goal, I do not allow myself to breathe in or out. When the opposing team kicks a field goal, I forcefully breathe out.

> During gymnastics competitions, one of the rules is that you can only have one earring in each ear. I first got my ears double-pierced when I was 14 and I couldn't take the new ones out because they were so new so I took the others out. Since that day and all throughout competing in college, I always competed with only my second piercings in.

I was once on a hitting streak so I wore the same unwashed undershirt under my jersey for the rest of the season.

I alway sit on the right side of the plane, in the aisle seat, when I'm on my way to see the Oakland Raiders play.

I can't watch a Cleveland Indians playoff game without my scrapbook that I made when I was 10 - 12 years old covering their 1995-97 playoff run. I was up until 2:00 a.m. during the 2016 post-season tearing my garage apart to find it.

I obsess over the number of pieces of candy I eat in a quarter/half of a game, the number of drinks I take during free throws or even the way I'm sitting in my seat.

The stories in this section are about times when superstition took hold and ended up creating some great memories. In one case, it created an actual positive result for the person telling that story. In the other, it helped create a bond between that individual and his peers. And in both cases, embracing superstition made the experience a better one.

MINE THAT BIRD

• • • • • • •

MATT ROBERTS
Director of Athletics
College of Charleston

I grew up playing all kinds of sports: soccer, football, baseball, basketball, you name it. And like anyone who has been involved in athletics their whole life, there are a lot of great stories I could tell you. But the one that stands out for me the most isn't about football or basketball. It's not about a game I played or one I worked. It's about a horse.

I've been to a lot of bucket list sporting events: the Super Bowl, World Series, NBA Finals, Masters, U.S. Opens, Final Fours, college football, and BCS games. None of them compare to the time I went to the Kentucky Derby.

It was 2009 and I was working at the University of Oklahoma. Bob Stoops, our head football coach, invited me to go to the Derby with him and a few others. Our group included Matt McMillen, the Director of Football Ops; Billy Ray Johnson, the Assistant AD for Ticket Operations; and Bob Cunningham, who was working for Billy Ray in the ticket office at the time.

When you go to the Kentucky Derby, it's not like going to a three-hour event where you're there and you're gone. You're there for two full days. The pageantry, the dress, the scene, the setting, the energy, the uniqueness of the sport itself, the fact that you can - as a college administrator, within NCAA rules - legally bet on the sport... the whole experience is amazing.

The first day was the Friday races that they call the Kentucky Oaks. We were having cigars and drinks, betting on the horses a little, and just having fun. I'm not an avid gambler and certainly not that knowledgeable about the sport of horse racing. We cared more about the experience than about the races.

The box we were sitting in was one of those old-school ones with folding chairs. I'm shooting the breeze with a guy named Jimmy Keith and all of a sudden I feel something on my face. I figure it's just water dripping from a gutter since it had rained earlier that morning, but when I go to wipe my face there's bird crap on my hand. I was pissed! It was all over my suit and the right side of my face. But as I'm scrambling to grab napkins and wipe my face off, Jimmy says, *Hey man, that's a great sign. Let's look and see who in the Derby has a name with the word bird in it or anything to do with a bird.*

I've been through enough games and events to be realistic about superstitions. What you wear, what you eat, the routines and everything that you do on the day of a game or day before the game have as much likelihood of being ineffective as they do of being effective. But superstition is in the fabric of sports. It's just part of it.

So we started flipping through the programs we'd gotten when we arrived. There were a few horses that had "bird" in their names, but one that drew my eye was Mine That Bird. The horse was a long shot, but I didn't care. Jimmy and I made a vow: *it's our secret and we're not telling anybody, but tomorrow we'll both bet Mine That Bird.*

The next day was Derby Day. On the way over to Churchill Downs, I happened to end up in the car with a local guy named Mike Meiners who had played football at Kentucky and lives in Louisville. He's a great guy, Mr. Kentucky - claims to know everything about horse racing. As he's telling us who we should bet on and what horses to avoid, he says: *Oh man, don't bet on Mine That Bird. That horse has a horrible pedigree, it's too small, it's got no chance. That's a sucker bet, the long shot. Don't waste your money, that horse has no chance of even placing.*

When it got close to post time for the Derby, I placed my bet on Mine That Bird anyway. I put down $20 across the board, which means betting Mine That Bird $20 to win, $20 to place, and $20 to show. If the horse wins, you win all three bets; if he comes in third, you at least get something for that $20 show bet. I bet on a few of the favorites too, like everybody else was doing.

Billy Ray had gotten us good seats right at the finish line, one level up from the floor. The only thing we could see was the straightaway and the first turn. As they got ready to bring the horses out, the trumpet call sent chills up my spine. The crowd was roaring as if somebody had just hit a grand slam to win game seven of the World Series. Then horses are in the gate and *bam!* the race starts. Here they come right in front of us heading to the first turn. There's one little horse that's trailing everybody by a long way. It's the number 8 horse, Mine That Bird. I didn't think much of it, because hey, what did I expect, it's a long shot, right?

So they go around and we can't really see the far side. We're just kind of waiting, wondering what's going to happen. I'm more worried about my other bets at this point. Then they make the final turn and all we can see is the pack. We can't tell them apart. But suddenly this one horse darts to the rail and takes off down the final straightaway. It was like he was a race car and just floored the gas.

Until the horse got about 100 yards away, I couldn't make out who it was. I wasn't paying attention to the video board. But then I see: it's Mine That Bird! He came out of nowhere. When he crossed the finish line to win, none of the others were even close.

I start going nuts. I'm pumping my fist, going crazy. The others are looking at me like I've lost my mind. I whip out the ticket and show it to them and they're like, *No way!* It was 40-something-to-one odds. I don't mind saying that my superstitious bet paid off pretty well.

It was an unbelievable trip. To be in one of the most iconic venues in the world for one of the most iconic sporting events in the world, and to put my faith in a long shot based on nothing more than superstition and see that long shot win… it was surreal. To this day, when the Derby's on I have a mint julep in one of the glasses I got at Churchill Downs so I can relive that experience.

VICTORY LUNCH

• • • • • • •

JOE PARKER
Director of Athletics
Colorado State University

When I was the Director of the Sooner Club at the University of Oklahoma, I was fortunate to have the opportunity to work with a really special group of people. We were all pretty early in our careers at that point and everyone was working tremendously hard because we didn't have a large staff. We were each kind of department heads but at the same time we were also the people who did all the day-to-day work: wearing the headsets, setting up or taking down tables and chairs, managing projects, and generally doing everything that needed to be done to execute events and manage games.

The first week of football season, we had all gotten to the point where we just needed a break. Somebody suggested that we go to lunch together, so a group of us ended up going to this sandwich shop in Norman called Bison Witches. I think it was me, Matt Trantham, Rick Hart, Kirby Hocutt, Jenny Bramer, and Chris Maxon. That weekend, OU got a great start to the season by beating UTEP 55-14. The following week we all kind of hit the wall again at the same point, probably on a Thursday or Friday, and decided to have lunch together again at Bison Witches. That Saturday, OU beat Arkansas State. A second victory! By week three of the season, we had kind of gotten into the routine of doing a group lunch late in the week at Bison Witches. That weekend: another game, another win. It wasn't until week four or five of the same thing happening that we started to think: *Hey, we might be onto something here!* We started joking around about how our weekly lunch was contributing to Saturday successes. It was just too much of a coincidence to disregard, right?

By week six or seven, we were fully committed to the concept and the Sooners were on an unbroken winning streak. We had started calling our weekly Bison Witches outing the *Victory Lunch* and it began to take on a life of its own. By then we had consistent attendance from everyone in the original group, because nobody wanted to be the one who missed a lunch and messed things up. We enjoyed the camaraderie of sharing those meals, but there was more to it than that. We had this sense of obligation not only to each other but also to the team and the fans. After all, we were helping make those wins happen every week. It might seem like a crazy superstition, but it got to where it felt like we had to do it – nobody wanted to be responsible for a Sooner loss.

By the end of the season, the *Victory Lunch* had become really serious business for us. It was do or die at that point. Even the week of the Big 12 Championship game, we made sure we had our scheduled lunch. Sure enough, the Sooners beat eighth-ranked Kansas State to take the title. Then, a few days before we left to go to Miami for the Orange Bowl we all made sure that we had a Bison Witches lunch together. And obviously it worked, because OU crushed Florida State in a 13-2 victory for the National Championship.

I don't consider myself a superstitious person, normally. When I was a student-athlete myself, I didn't have any special rituals or anything. I've never had a lucky hat. But that season, there was just something different about the *Victory Lunch*. In our jobs, we put a lot of time and energy into making game day special for other people. The *Victory Lunch* tradition that season was something we kind of did for ourselves - to celebrate the relationships we were building with one another, to take a break from the crazy work experience we were having, and of course to help our team keep winning.

(7)
CHAPTER SEVEN
WE'RE ALL CHANTICLEERS

"**Nobody roots for Goliath.**"
- Wilt Chamberlain

Underdog : noun
a competitor thought to have little chance in a fight or contest

According to Anoosh Chakelian from a 2011 article in *The Telegraph*,

> *"the origin of the term 'underdog' can be discovered in the murky depths of ship-building history. Planks of wood labeled 'dogs' would be placed over a pit, and one happy ship-builder would saw from above, while the other would have to stand in the pit, sawing from below, becoming covered in sawdust, but doing an equal amount of the work. Weeping. The man above was the 'overdog', and the man below, the 'underdog'. Why the planks were called 'dogs', we'll never know."*

Other articles I found said the term comes from dogfighting when the presumed winner was called the "top dog" and the presumed loser, therefore, would be the "under dog."

Honestly, I like the first story better and though I haven't spent hours researching which one is more historically accurate, for some reason it's the ship-building story that rings more true for me. Maybe that's just because that origin of the term fits better with my understanding of what a true underdog is.

Rooting for the Underdog

Think about the last time you were watching a sporting event in which you didn't really care who won. Remove from consideration any game where your alma mater or favorite team was playing because you're obviously biased toward them. On the flip side, remove any game in which your ex's favorite team was playing because, in that situation, you most definitely want that team to lose.

So those situations aside, when was the last time you were watching an event where there was an obvious underdog and you did not pull for them? When was the last time you saw a team that had been historically underwhelming, had scraped and clawed to achieve a place alongside a historical powerhouse, had overcome adversity to be in that game in the first place, were the odds-on underdogs... and you cheered for the favorite to win?

A few of you fall into that camp. Some of you only ever cheer for the team that gives you the best shot of saying that your team won. The rest of us aren't like you. We're decent human beings. We don't kick puppies or push old ladies down while they're trying to cross the street. And we definitely pull for the underdogs.

The Chanticleers

Before I even move on to the next part, can we just all agree that a Chanticleer is one of the coolest sports mascots of all time? There's nothing better than out-of-the-ordinary team names and the Coastal Carolina Chanticleers takes the cake. Do you know what a chanticleer is? It's a rooster.

So what's more fun than rooting for the underdog? Yep, you guessed it: rooting for an underdog with an amazing mascot. We had the opportunity to cheer for an underdog with an amazing mascot in the 2016 College World Series as the Coastal Carolina Chanticleers took on the Arizona Wildcats.

Now, nothing against the U of A, of course. Old Hat has worked with Arizona on many projects and I have so much respect for the university, their athletic program and the people who work there. However, in this particular competition of winning over disinterested third-party fans, Arizona had no chance. Arizona may be a lot of things but an underdog, they are not. Let's just look at some things that take them out of the running for underdog consideration:

- Power 5 School
- Historically very good in baseball
- 4 previous baseball national championships
- National recognition as a top athletic program
- They're "wildcats," of all things

Now, I don't know exactly how many schools out there call themselves the Wildcats, but out of 347 D1 programs out there, I'm pretty sure that about 342 of them are the Wildcats. That's not scientific so don't quote me on that, but it's close. And while there's nothing wrong with being the Wildcats, when it comes down to choosing who we're cheering for in the CWS and it's between the Power 5, historically-dominant Wildcats and the underdog, Cinderella-team Chanticleers, sports fans flock to the roosters.

That's exactly what the majority of the nation did. I'm not a huge college baseball aficionado. I've been known to skip a CWS or two in my time, especially if the teams playing in it are not in my circle of favorites, but the entire country was watching the Chanticleers rise through the rankings. We watched them win time after time and as fans of the underdog, we found ourselves invested in a team that we not only had no affiliation with, we couldn't even tell you what town Coastal Carolina University was in.

It's Conway, South Carolina, by the way.

So when our newly beloved Chanticleers won it all, we were ecstatic. We celebrated. We were elated. We were all things that begin with an "e" and/or rhyme with celebrated.

And then we asked ourselves why in the world we were so happy that the Coastal Carolina Chanticleers won the College World Series.

The World is a Wildcat

We pull for the underdog because all of us feel that on some level, we are the underdogs. At some point in life, we've all been the guy standing in the pit, sawing from below and getting covered in sawdust. Very few of us can claim that we were never on a team that was the underdog. But most of us can think of a time when we overcame adversity to achieve something great. So we're always pulling for others to do the same.

It doesn't only apply to sports. I was the underdog when I left my job at Oklahoma Athletics to start my own company. I had to overcome great odds to be successful. I had to sacrifice a lot and work my tail off. I was going up against big agencies that had a lot of financial backing and a history of working with top clients. It was Zac vs. the Wildcats. I was a Chanticleer.

I think we can all recall many times when we were the underdogs. And because we've been there – because many times we probably lost that fight and walked away from it covered in sawdust – anytime we see another underdog we identify with them. We relate to them. So when they have success, even if we never attended school there or even knew where that team was located before we sat down to watch that game, we feel like we have success. When they win, we win.

The world is a Wildcat. And at some point, we're all Chanticleers.

BEAT NAVY!

• • • • • • •

STEPHANIE MENIO
Senior Woman Administrator
United States Military Academy

There's a long tradition of friendly rivalry between the United States Military Academy and the United States Naval Academy, and every year the highlight of that rivalry is the Army-Navy football game. If you say Go Army to a cadet or former cadet, the response is always *Beat Navy!* whether you're talking about football or not.

West Point had lost every Army-Navy game since 2001. Our 14-year losing streak was all College Game Day and the rest of the media talked about prior to this year's Army-Navy game. That type of record can take a toll on any organization and its fans but I think it was especially difficult for us as a service academy. We're not just developing athletes, we're developing future officers and future leaders, and that requires a winning mindset. Our Superintendent always talks about how the Army can't come in second. We have to come in first because lives depend on it.

One of the unique things about West Point is that every cadet is an athlete because athletics is a huge component of developing leadership skills. We always say Macarthur's quote: *Upon the fields of friendly strife Are sown the seeds That, upon other fields, on other days, Will bear the fruits of victory.* Everything we do is focused on helping the cadets develop mental toughness and the will to win. Our student-athletes have a different experience than students at other schools. During the academic year, they're often up at

5:30 in the morning to get in a lift before their first formation, then they're in classes and other mandatory activities from 7:30 a.m. until 3:00 p.m. Athletics time is 3:00 p.m. to 6:30 p.m., then the cadets are required to attend dinner and study until Taps. They have training events on many weekends and during the summers they're on three-week rotations for training or summer classes. The skills our athletes are learning when they stand up in front of the team to motivate their fellow players are some of the same skills they'll use when leading soldiers a few months after graduation.

A lot of blood, sweat and tears went into revamping our football program and undertaking an institutional culture change to support it. Keep in mind, when we hire coaches at West Point it's like: *Hey, you're going to be coaching a team but you're also going to be recruiting and developing the leaders of our Army and our nation.* Where else does your football coach have to interview in the Pentagon for their job? Coming into this year's Army-Navy game, we just had this feeling that we were going to win. We had to win! But it was something nobody wanted to talk about, because you didn't want to jeopardize the possibility.

The game itself is always a powerful experience thanks to all the tradition associated with it. This year we added to the sense of history with special uniforms that represented the 82nd Airborne Division's paratroopers who jumped into World War II. Those guys were fearless and they were instrumental in winning a great victory, so paying homage to them was really inspirational for all of us.

Normally, my role at West Point is to handle game presentation like video boards and on-field recognition, but because it was Navy's year to host I was mostly a spectator. It was gut-wrenching to do nothing but watch from the sidelines. As the lead switched back and forth, the intensity in the stadium was unbelievable. I could barely stand to watch the game so I just paced back and forth, focusing on our cadets' reactions. When we were up by three points in the second half, I went into the cheerleaders' locker room to gather myself for a few seconds. When I came back out we were losing and I kept thinking, *This cannot happen. This cannot happen! We have to win this game.* In the fourth quarter I remember looking over and seeing our Chaplain kneeling and praying behind the team, then one of the players pulling him up and saying, *Father Matt, you've got to see this! We're going to win this game!*

When the clock hit zero, the score was 21-17 in our favor and a tidal wave of cadets came over the railing to storm the field. They were headed straight toward me and I had a split second to make my decision: either go up against the wall to avoid getting trampled or join them. So of course I joined them. As the momentum of the cadets carried me forward onto the field, the elation all around me was overwhelming. Current cadets and old grads were jumping up and down together; former athletes were running past me to join our players; grown men were weeping in the stands. On the screen they showed a shot of soldiers deployed overseas who had stayed up through the middle of the night to watch the game and they were going crazy celebrating. All the pain of the past 14 seasons was released with the joy of finally achieving victory. I had never seen or experienced anything like it.

Singing the alma mater at the end of the game is a huge part of the Army-Navy tradition. Both teams sing, but the order in which they sing is determined by the game's outcome. The victor gets to sing second. As they played Navy's alma mater, everyone fell silent and faced the Navy's band to pay their respects. Then we all turned toward our band for the playing of our alma mater, but our band wasn't there. They had rushed the field with everyone else! It was just a couple of tubas and the Band Director standing there waving his arms like: *I don't even know what to do. I'm just going to pretend there are people here.* The Corps sang the alma mater from the field and even though it was a little off-tempo it was a beautiful sound. Hearing everybody shout *Beat Navy!* at the end gave me goosebumps.

When our team went to the locker room after the game, they didn't start celebrating immediately. One of our players, Brandon Jackson, had died in a car accident after our game on September 11, 2016 so the team brought his mom down to the locker room after the game. Every member of the team had worn a #28 helmet decal in Brandon's memory throughout the season. His loss had been really difficult for the entire team and it was really important to them to be able to honor his family with such a big win.

Army's victory in the 2016 Army-Navy game was a story for the ages. I think everybody expected there to be this huge celebration afterward but instead we all just sat and looked at each other in shock that it had really happened. Everybody was just emotionally drained and needed time to process the moment. You could say it's just a football game, but that event represents so much more. The U.S. Military Academy symbolizes American history and the strength of our nation. When our players step on that field they're not just playing for West Point, they're playing for the entire United States Army. We're honoring all who have served and boosting the morale of thousands. All those years of enduring so many losses both on the football field and off made our victory that much sweeter.

CINDERELLA

• • • • • • •

JEFF COMPHER
Director of Athletics
East Carolina University

In 2012, I was working as the Director of Athletics at Northern Illinois University. Our football team had played really well all season and we made it into the Mid-American Conference (MAC) Championship Game in Detroit. The MAC was a non-automatic qualifying conference, which meant that winning the conference didn't necessarily mean you'd have the chance to go to a Bowl Championship Series game. To qualify for a bowl game, the MAC Conference Champion had to finish 16th or higher in the BCS ranking and be ranked ahead of at least one automatically qualifying conference champion.

Before we went to Detroit, I remember joking with MAC Commissioner Jon Steinbrecher about the possibility of getting into a bowl game. *Jon, I said, we've had a pretty good year. If there's any chance of us getting picked for a bowl game, it would be really nice to go somewhere warm.* Northern Illinois isn't exactly a great place to be in the winter and visiting Detroit for MAC wasn't much better!

Going into the MAC Championship Game we were ranked 19th. Our opponent was No. 18 Kent State, and both teams put everything they had on the line. It was a tough game that went into double overtime, but we finally beat Kent State 44-37. That victory gave us the highest number of regular season wins in our program's 113-year history and moved us up to

15th in the rankings, which meant we might just have a chance at a bowl game depending on how some of the other conference champions did. But as I was driving back from the game, I received a call from our football coach Dave Doeren. He said, *Jeff, I've accepted the job at NC State University. I need to tell the team today because they're picking me up to fly me to Raleigh.*

Less than 48 hours later we were scheduled to announce our new head coach. That morning, I got a call from the MAC Commissioner. He said, *Hey Jeff, you know how you said you wanted to go someplace warm? Congratulations, you're going to the Orange Bowl!* We had edged out Big East Champion Louisville in the BCS rankings. When Jon gave me the news I was nearly overcome with tears because it was such a seminal moment for our university, for our athletics program and specifically for our football program. I will never forget that feeling. I thanked Jon profusely because I knew how much he must have lobbied for us to get that opportunity. It was the first time a MAC team had ever qualified for a major bowl game and it was the first major bowl appearance in NIU's history.

When I got off the phone, I told one of my assistants: *Hey, just out of the blue, could you send somebody to the store to grab a couple cases of oranges?* They looked at me like I was crazy. I said, *Just humor me. Go to the store and get some oranges, but don't send any of our coaches because people will start to wonder what we're up to.* We ended up getting two cases of oranges, and after the ceremony recognizing co-offensive coordinator Rod Carey as our new head coach, we gave the oranges out to our coaches, players, and the media as part of the announcement that we would be going to the Orange Bowl. It was a madhouse! It was one of those emotional times where you have to pinch yourself to make sure it's real and you just keep thinking, *Is this really happening?* It was truly a special day.

At first ESPN was saying things like, *They don't deserve it, they don't belong there,* but the rest of the media rallied behind us. That's no small thing when you're in a market like Chicago. Suddenly we were the best team in the entire state of Illinois and we were getting front page articles in every newspaper in the state. People who had never cheered for us before were saying, *It's the best thing ever, it's a Cinderella story!* The university lit up our athletic facilities in orange lights, put up billboards all over the city, placed signs on buses and took out full-page ads. We had autograph signings and alumni events in downtown Chicago. We did everything we could to maximize our exposure both locally and nationally, and the positive response we got was overwhelming. There was an unbelievable sense of pride among our alumni and anyone who was affiliated with the university in any way.

I think we ended up taking 6,000 or 7,000 people to the game. It was incredible to have so many members of our fan base travel so far to watch us play. Even though we didn't end up winning the Orange Bowl, the attention it brought to NIU really legitimized us as a football team and as an athletic program. That season had a lasting impact on the entire university. It takes many people and many years to build a program to that point, so when you get to see it come together in a storybook way it's an unforgettable experience.

JAMES JUSTICE DAY

• • • • • • •

TRACIE HITZ
Director of Championships and Alliances
NCAA

Martin Methodist College, an 800 person college in Pulaski, Tennessee, had a basketball player they wanted to get into the 2012 State Farm® College Slam Dunk & 3 Point Championships. Jeff Bain, the Director of Athletics at Martin Methodist, nominated his player James Justice as a "Dark Horse Dunker" entrant, which was still fairly new at the time. Basically, it's a way for under-the-radar basketball players to earn the chance to compete in the Slam Dunk Contest at the NCAA Final Four through a bracket-style social media matchup.

Jeff's nominee was a 5'9" guard. James is not as tall as your average player, but he could dunk a basketball and he definitely has a lot of heart. Jeff was confident that James would surprise people if they could just convince enough fans to vote for him to then give him that chance.

The deck seemed to be stacked against him as he struggled to get votes in the Dark Horse Dunker voting contest on Facebook because bigger and better programs with more recognition commanded the lead. It was to be expected since James was a relatively unknown player from a little-known school. I was working at Old Hat Creative at the time, and I didn't know who James was when Jeff reached out to us for help getting James into the spotlight. He didn't have the budget necessary for a full campaign, but at Old Hat we saw it as an opportunity to have some fun, let our creativity run wild and help the underdog. I love a good underdog story.

We designed all kinds of marketing collateral to promote James. I told Jeff, *You need to do this, this, and this; you need to go to Nashville, you need to go to the media, you need to create this, you need to get this social media out there.* Jeff was on board to follow my recommendations and James ended up winning his bracket with something like 51 percent of the vote. He barely squeaked by but he made it!

The contest went to the next round –the final round– and again, James was getting pummeled in the voting. So we went back and did even more to get James' name and story out there. James was a good kid with a huge heart and a great story, so we knew if we could get enough people talking about him, he'd be able to get the votes he needed. I mean, we were talking about a kid who's 5'9" and dunking!

We did a lot on social media and knew that a video promoting James would help draw attention to his talent and his personality. Unfortunately, James' highlight reels included footage that was probably shot on a phone or a hand-held camera. The footage was really shaky, especially compared to the highlight reels that were created for student-athletes from bigger programs. We knew we had to do more to make James' video stand out, so our intern wrote and recorded a song about James and laid it over the video. The lyrics went something like *James Justice, fight for justice. Stands just five foot nine as his dunks be unmercifully be pilin' up. Up, vertically he's flyin' up, up. Let's get this kid to New Orleans 'cuz this guy's dunks are just obscenely beautiful. James Justice.* After that, no one paid attention to how poor the highlight footage was, they loved that this guy had his own song and that he could dunk. The song got people talking about him, and more people started watching his video, including the Nashville media. With this added reach, James ended up winning the Facebook vote by a very small margin again.

I remember saying, *Oh my gosh, we just won! James made it into the contest as a dark horse entrant!* We were thrilled that James would get his chance to compete in the dunk contest at the Final Four, but then Jeff said, *I can't afford to send him to New Orleans. That's on the school and we don't have the money to do it.* There was no way Jeff and I were going to let James miss this once-in-a-lifetime opportunity. So we put together a fundraising plan that included our intern designing an exclusive James Justice t-shirt. Martin Methodist printed the t-shirts and sold them as part of a fundraiser that got James to New Orleans so he could continue telling his underdog story.

It was the first time in the contest's history that fan votes via Twitter counted as part of the official judging for the dunk contest, so the number of people following his story was amplified. Plus, the arena at Tulane University was sold out for the event. Once the crowd saw James in action, they couldn't get enough of him. I remember watching the contest on TV and every time he made a dunk, the crowd went a little crazier. James' smile and genuine excitement to be competing just fueled the crowd even more. Here is a guy who went from an unknown basketball player in Pulaski, Tennessee to the crowd favorite in a matter of days. James took home the Slam Dunk title with a between the legs alley-oop. The fans were going completely nuts, and other competitors even ran off the bench to show their respect. When he lifted the title belt and flashed that smile, the place erupted again. It wasn't just because he overcame so many odds and proved he could dunk, it was also because people had fallen in love with this truly amazing person.

Watching him on TV was the moment I realized, *Oh my gosh, I helped make that happen.* Here's a guy who no one thinks will even make it into a dunk contest at the Final Four, and then he ends up winning it. It was a special moment because the Pulaski community believed in him which led the Old Hat Creative team to believe in him, so the fans then started to believe in him. He showed everybody that it doesn't matter where you come from or what you look like, you can become a champion if you put your heart and soul into it. All he needed was the chance to do it.

A couple of months later, I went to Pulaski and was blown away when I saw a billboard that had his smiling face next to the text that said "James Justice Day." They named a day after him in Pulaski, Tennessee! To be able to help such a deserving kid at a small school do something so huge on a national stage was definitely my favorite moment working in the sports industry. It was a true underdog story.

DO THE IMPOSSIBLE

• • • • • • •

LEAH BEASLEY
*Associate Athletic Director
of Marketing and Fan Engagement*
Mississippi State University

Like a lot of people who are involved in college athletics, I grew up with a love of sports. Some of my earliest memories are watching games on TV with my dad; that was always our special daddy-daughter time. As I got older, I started playing soccer, basketball and softball. They didn't have separate girls' programs where I grew up, so the girls played on the same teams as the boys. Because of that, I always felt like I had to work harder just to prove myself.

I think that's why I've always identified with the underdog. There's something about their attitude that just resonates with me: they know they're going to have to outwork everyone else and they're not afraid to give that extra effort. Every time I hear the term underdog, I picture bulldogs. Maybe it's because I was raised a Louisiana Tech Bulldog fan, graduated from Louisiana Tech and currently work with the Mississippi State Bull-dogs. If you think about bulldogs, their personality really does fit with the idea of the underdog: they might not have the most impressive stature but they've got grit, they're hard-nosed, and they're tenacious. No matter what the odds, they don't give up.

One of the moments that really stands out for me is the 2004 Louisiana Tech – Fresno State football game. That was always a big rivalry game in the Western Athletic Conference because we had the same mascot, the Bulldogs. They called it the "Battle for the Bone," and in the three years since the series had started, Louisiana Tech had never won. Coming into the game that year, Fresno State was ranked #17 and they were undefeated. It was the first time we'd ever had a ranked opponent at our stadium! I remember being at the stadium for the game with my sister, my now brother-in-law, and another friend. We were sitting on the east side in the student section and it was absolutely freezing. It doesn't snow very often in Ruston, Louisiana but it was snowing that day. It was miserable, and a lot of people left early because they didn't think we stood a chance against Fresno. As a softball player at Louisiana Tech, I had developed a bond with many of the football players. Those were my friends on the field and I wasn't going to leave early and abandon them. At the very end we won 28-21 and everyone went crazy! We hadn't just beaten a ranked team, we hadn't just beaten an undefeated team, we had beaten our undefeated ranked rival at home on our own turf! People rushed the field and started tearing down the goalposts.

I had never seen anything like it. At first I was like, *Wait, what's happening?!* It was surreal. That's something that just doesn't happen at Louisiana Tech… at least, not when I was growing up! But then the realization of our victory hit me like a wave and I just wanted to rush the field with everyone else. We were sitting kind of high up in the stadium, so we weren't able to get down to the field. I remember being really upset because I wanted to be on that field so badly! Seeing other folks I knew down on the field, folks who were working the game, made me think: *I want to be in it, how can I be IN it?* That was a pivotal moment for me.

Fast-forward a few years to 2008, when I was Assistant Athletic Director for Marketing at Louisiana Tech. At the start of the football season that year, Mississippi State actually came to Ruston for a game. That was a big deal: it was the first time an SEC team had traveled to Louisiana Tech for a game since 1908. We put a lot of work into preparing for the game and getting our fans to come out for it, even though we weren't expected to win or even be able to keep up with them. We hadn't beaten a BCS conference team in five years but that didn't matter to us or our fans. Everyone knew that we would go out there and play our hardest.

The game took place in August and it was really hot outside. We had one of the largest crowds we'd ever had for a home game and everyone was just burning up. It was almost as miserable as that cold 2004 game but in the extreme opposite way. At halftime, Mississippi State was leading but in the third quarter our team managed to catch three interceptions. The tide started to turn and the crowd was in a frenzy. We ended up winning 22-14, and it was one of the most incredible and unexpected upsets ever!

People in the stands were losing their minds and trying to rush the field. This time, I wasn't way up in the nosebleed section of the stands! I remember being in a corner of the south end zone where the final drive ended. I threw my headset off, threw my script out, and just ran and yelled. I was completely caught up in the moment! After a few minutes of celebrating, I was like, *Oh my gosh, I have a job to do. Okay, hope nobody saw that,* and pulled myself together.

When you're an underdog, you might not always achieve the optimal outcome but you always work your hardest. I think that's something other people notice and respect. When an individual or team like that does finally win, it's an amazing feeling. It makes you realize that hard work really does pay off and that sometimes, with a little luck, you can do the impossible.

A MYSTICAL THING

• • • • • • •

MATT HOGUE
Director of Athletics
Coastal Carolina University

As a kid, I remember picking up the Charlotte Observer the day after the selections for the NCAA Tournament and cutting the bracket out of the paper. Back then if you didn't cut the bracket out of the paper on Monday, there wouldn't be another chance to get your hands on a bracket until they printed one for the Final Four. It was one of those things that was kind of magical about following college basketball at that time.

For me, there was a certain mysticism to the Tournament. I loved following the teams and I knew the names of all the players; I even knew the theme music for the broadcast. One of my most vivid memories is of NC State beating Houston to win the championship in 1983. NC State had a good team that year but they'd lost their best player, Dereck Whittenburg, to an injury early in the season. They weren't seen as much of a contender but I cheered for them anyway. The drama and romanticism of NC State's unexpected run to the top was incredibly exciting to follow! I remember sitting in my living room with my dad and a buddy of his, watching the ball go into the air for the final shot of the championship game.

I think a lot of us root for the underdog because it's what we can identify with. There's a moment where most of us realize we aren't good enough to play at a higher level; that we'll never be much more than weekend warriors or weekend softball players. Nonetheless, we can still identify with the challenges and the odds that have to be overcome for somebody to make it to the top, and it's inspiring when we see a person or team whose success kind of goes against the system. I think we all innately want to try to accomplish things that people say we can't accomplish. Seeing it happen for somebody else creates a certain level of hope in us.

As an adult, one of my greatest experiences was being part of an underdog story. Coastal Carolina wasn't known as an athletic powerhouse, and I think some of our greatest victories today started with our baseball program playing at the Regional in Georgia in 2001. After an incredible back-and-forth we came up short in the regional final against the Bulldogs after future Major Leaguer Jeff Keppinger hit his third home run of the day, but we began to realize, *If we can do what we need to do to build this program, little by little, we can get to that level. Our program could do this! Our program could go the distance in this sport.* Over the years since then, I've developed a great bond with former CCU Coach John Vrooman and his successor Coach Gary Gilmore as they have worked to build our baseball program. I had a small part in that growth, but I always felt like I was an advocate for the program. Finally, this past year, we made it to the College World Series.

For a kid who ordered College World Series Programs in the early '80s, being in Omaha with the team that ended up winning the National Championship in 2016 was indescribable. I actually called the final inning, and I remember trying to get down to the field as fast as I could after the last pitch. As I dropped my headset and rushed to join the celebration, everything we had gone through to get to that moment flashed through my mind: the close calls, the tough games, the Regionals that didn't go our way, the Super-Regionals where we came up a little bit short; just the grind, the effort, and the continuous pursuit of our goal. I experienced a tremendous feeling of satisfaction that we were finally able to overcome those barriers. When I got down to the field, I immediately found Gilly and gave him a bear hug that lasted two or three minutes. The emotion was just overwhelming. I also shared a moment with John and we both nearly broke down in tears because we knew the role he had played in getting us to that moment. We all took pictures with the trophy on the field and it's one of those moments that will forever have a kind of pureness to it. I was with my family, I was with people that I've worked hard with and cared about most in this business, and we had accomplished our ultimate goal.

When I look back, I think it's all tied together. From being a kid watching NC State unexpectedly win the NCAA Tournament to being part of Coastal Carolina's achievement of a seemingly impossible goal, I think my experiences have taught me that the challenges are what make winning so powerful. Winning is always memorable, but I think it means the most when you've fought hard and invested so much of yourself to reach that accomplishment. When a team seizes an opportunity to do something others don't think they can do, it can be a mystical thing to experience.

THIRD QUARTER
THE TEAM

The first known use of the word "team," in reference to a group of individuals working together for a specific purpose, dates back to the 1520s. Back then, it was more likely used to refer to a team of oxen used to pull a plow. Or a team of soldiers storming a castle. Or a team of individuals pouring molten lead onto a team of soldiers that were storming a castle before returning to their fields so their team of oxen could pull their team of plows. Point being, for nearly 500 years now, the concept of a team has referred to a group of people or animals, all working together to achieve a common goal.

Fast forward half a millennia and we are inundated with "team" on a daily basis. We join teams at school and at work. We talk about it being a "team effort." We say, *There's no 'i' in team!* and we have corporate team building exercises and retreats that cost companies millions of dollars a year. There is an entire industry built around the idea of team building and there are professional speakers that make their living speaking on the subject. Needless to say, it seems like being on a team is one of the most important things a person can be these days. Being accused of not being a "team player" (a term dating back to 1886, by the way) is akin to being accused of clubbing baby polar bears.

As much as the term is used in reference to things outside the sports world, in the 21st century "team" is synonymous with sports. We all want our kids in sports so they can learn the "team mentality." We aren't nearly as proud to be on the office party planning team as we are the church softball team. And no one wonders what we're talking about when we ask, *What team ya pullin' for next week, Jimmy?* Jimmy knows we're asking about whatever big game is coming up.

Bo Schembechler famously said, *No man is more important than The Team. No coach is more important than The Team. The Team, The Team, The Team.*

We all want to be on a team and be a team player. And no teams are more important to us than our sports teams. The stories in the Third Quarter of this book are about team members. However, they are not just about the athletes. There are three types of people that must work together to achieve success in sports: athletes, coaches and fans. You cannot have a successful sports program without the athletes, obviously. I think the athletes would agree they cannot be successful without coaches. And none of it would be possible if it weren't for the fans.

This section is about all of those different team members: how sports affects them and how they have the opportunity to affect sports in a positive way.

8

CHAPTER EIGHT
THE BEST INTEREST

> **An investment in knowledge pays the best interest.**
> *- Benjamin Franklin*

According to the NCAA, each year there are more than 480,000 student-athletes competing on more than 19,000 collegiate teams through the three divisions of the NCAA. Of those student-athletes, more than half receive some level of financial aid to help cover the cost of their education. Each year, that amounts to more than $2.7 billion in scholarships for student-athletes, many of whom would not have access to a college education without athletics. Additionally, the NAIA provides opportunities for another 65,000 student-athletes annually, awarding more than $500 million in scholarship money.

Unfortunately, no data exists on student-athletes who would not be able to receive a college education without the benefit of an athletic scholarship. It should be assumed, however, that collegiate athletics provides that benefit to a lot of people who would otherwise never have had that opportunity. Beyond that, there are many others who may have gone to college but without athletics, would have graduated with a mound of debt. The point of all of this is to say that more than half of the 500,000 collegiate student-athletes competing each year are getting all or some of their education paid for. However, what collegiate athletics provides in the way of educational benefits is far beyond the almost $3 billion it spends on scholarships annually.

The monetary value of the educational opportunities athletics provides is immeasurable. But for argument's sake, let's try. Working in round numbers, let's say that there are 500,000 student-athletes enrolled each year and that half of them are on athletic scholarships. That's 250,000 young men and women, one-fourth of whom will graduate each year (assuming that one-fourth are freshmen, one-fourth are sophomores, and so on). So we have approximately 62,500 student-athletes graduating each year whose education was paid for by the NCAA or NAIA.

According to *Time.com,* a college graduate in 2016 received an average starting salary of just above $50,000. Assuming they work at least 40 years after they graduate and without taking into account any pay increases, the dollar value of each student-athlete's education is $2 million over their lifetime. Multiply that by the number graduating each year and you have a value of $125 billion in educational benefits provided by athletics *every single year.*

That's just what the student-athlete gains from a financial perspective, though. Reducing the benefit of what athletics truly provides young people to a dollar figure does not do justice to how sports shapes their lives. There are countless intangible benefits a student-athlete receives through their athletics experience as well. A home, a family, confidence and a sense of belonging are just a few things that being a part of an athletic program provides that some of these athletes would not have access to otherwise.

Chapter 8 highlights the ways athletics shapes the lives of athletes from an educational and formative perspective. It's important to note that while these stories highlight collegiate student-athletes specifically, the education, the sense of belonging and the confidence one gains from competing in sports is something that is applicable from Little League on up.

AKEEM JUDD

• • • • • • •

ROSS BJORK
Vice Chancellor for Intercollegiate Athletics
University of Mississippi

Like any other program, we have a vision statement and a purpose statement. We have core values. We have a commitment to developing our students to their full potential through athletics. Those are things everybody puts up all over their buildings, but nothing brings the point home like seeing it really happen.

There's a young man who was a running back for us. He was a junior college transfer from Georgia Military Institute and red-shirted before playing his last two years at Ole Miss. His name is Akeem Judd and he's from Durham, North Carolina.

When most people hear Durham, North Carolina, they think of Duke University. Duke's a nice place but other parts of Durham can be pretty rough, especially the area where Akeem grew up. Akeem's parents were sort of in and out of his life. His dad would come and go, so his mom raised him and his siblings. She worked all the time and battled depression throughout her life, which meant she often just wasn't around. It was tough on Akeem.

At some point, somebody threw Akeem a football and he realized he was pretty athletic. He started playing the game as a young man and continued to play in high school. But his sophomore year, he was going to drop out. Hardly anybody in his neighborhood finished high school. He was like, *I'm just going to do what everybody else does.* He had gotten into a little drug dealing. One night when he was on his way to his girlfriend's house, some-body mistook him for another person and shot at him in his own neighbor-hood. Finally, his older brother grabbed him and said, *Man, you can't drop out. You have to finish school.*

Not too long after that, Akeem was visiting with his high school coun-selor and told her that he hadn't eaten in days. She asked him some ques-tions and got to know more of his story. She and her husband decided to bring Akeem into their home and ended up basically adopting him. He began calling Mr. and Mrs. Bullock his mom and dad.

We, at Ole Miss, discovered Akeem Judd kind of by accident. We were going to Georgia Military Institute to look at another kid as a possible transfer. While we were down there, we saw this running back. We're like, *Man, this guy's pretty good. Who is this kid?* Even before we knew much about Akeem's background, we knew he had substance.

There are a lot of naysayers who criticize the money that's in the in-dustry, how much coaches make and how much we pour into facilities. Yet those things are all part of what we do to create opportunities for kids like Akeem. Every time I see Akeem, he looks at me and says, *Mr. Ross, thank you. Thanks for the resources, thanks for giving me a chance. I love you guys, I love our coaches.* And when you see him smile, you know how much he means it. He's appreciative that sports helped save him. If not for athletics and an education, Akeem Judd may not even be alive today.

Throughout all the turmoil in Akeem's life, the one thing he held onto was football. It gave him something good to focus on and it gave him a rea-son to keep moving forward. If Akeem didn't have athletics, he might still be involved in drugs. He'd probably be in a gang, or he may not even be here at this point. He definitely wouldn't have gone to college. But football was an avenue for him to overcome his setting.

Looking at it from that perspective makes you realize: *Man, this is what we do. This is the impact that an athletic program, an education, a recruiting moment, can have on somebody's life.* When something like that happens, you want to bottle it and make sure that it lives on as part of your platform forever, because that's why we're here.

There are a million Akeem Judd stories out there about kids who made it. There are also the same number of stories where kids didn't make it be-cause they did not seize the moment or take advantage of their opportuni-ties. But Akeem did and we're better off for it as an institution; he's better off for it as a person. Akeem earned his degree here in December 2016, and that's ultimately what will define his life going forward. He'll try to play at the next level but he also knows that his degree means more than playing football.

You want to talk about having a purpose statement and what it means throughout athletics, that's it in a nutshell. There's no better man than Akeem Judd to have this platform and this opportunity to better himself. It's a story we like to tell, because stories like these do not get the attention they deserve.

A LASTING IMPACT

• • • • • • •

LEE DE LEON
Director of Athletics
Abilene Christian University

At Abilene Christian University, we hold a special reception at the end of every semester for student-athletes who are graduating. Each time, I welcome everybody and then I say, *Raise your hand if you're the first person in your family to graduate from college.* It's always a risk, because I never know if anyone will raise their hand. I always hope that somebody does, because it's such a powerful moment to see those hands go into the air. Without fail, each time I've done that there have been at least five hands raised. I always tell those graduates, *You just changed the standard of what people are going to do educationally in your families for generations. By being the first one to graduate from college you've created a legacy. You haven't just changed the trajectory of your own life, you've changed the future for everyone in your family who comes after you.* That's always my favorite moment, because seeing the impact we've been able to have on entire families is such an amazing thing.

I've always valued the educational opportunities we're able to provide for our student-athletes, but even I never realized how much those scholarships sometimes mean to these kids. We had a young man named Carlton LaFrance on our football team last semester. He decided to quit the team mid-season, which was really frustrating and disappointing. We thought he was gone for good and had no desire to come back to ACU. We changed coaches and suddenly found out that Carlton had enrolled for the next semester. He hadn't talked to us about coming back to the team, so I gave him a call and asked him what his plans were. He told me, *Yeah, I'd just like to come back and stay in school.* I said, *Well, we thought you quit so we kind of moved on but I'll talk to Coach Dorrel, our new football coach.* Coach and I decided to go ahead and honor Carlton's scholarship for the semester even though he wasn't on the team anymore, just to give him the opportunity to keep going to class. Later that semester, Carlton came into my office. He said, *Man, I'm so thankful you guys let me back in school because I was going to be homeless this semester.* He had his head down and was kind of mumbling so I wasn't sure I had heard him right. I said, *What?! What did you just say?* He told me, Y*eah, I didn't have a place to live so if you guys hadn't let me come back and go to class and live on campus I wasn't going to have anywhere to live.* It just broke my heart. I had no idea how much he depended on that scholarship and the small living stipend we provide for our student-athletes.

If not for athletics, Carlton would have been homeless. Even though he chose not to stay with our program, through sports he was able to get an education and avoid living on the streets. If not for athletics, so many other young men and women would never have the opportunity to be the first one in their family to go to college, changing the course of lives for generations to come. To me, those stories say the most about the power of college athletics. Through the programs we run, we make a lasting impact on people's lives.

CEREMONY FOR ONE

• • • • • • •

JEFF BAIN
Athletic Director
Martin Methodist College

We had a young man named Chauncey Shelton on the basketball team at Martin Methodist College. Chauncey was an African-American student-athlete from Detroit. He was a great guy and a very good basketball player, just one of those really likable kids.

When Chauncey had one year of basketball eligibility remaining, he still had two years left to go before he would have enough credits to graduate. I brought Chauncey into my office and said, *Chauncey, I know you only have one year left to play. Will you promise me that you'll stay a fifth year and get your degree if we make you a student assistant and give you a scholarship to you for that final year?* He replied, *I want to graduate. Nobody in my family has ever graduated from a four-year school. I want to be the first because I have a little sister that's seven years old and I want her to be able to do it too.*

I told Chauncey I would make a deal with him. *If you'll promise me you'll stick with it and graduate, I promise that we'll scholarship you to get your diploma. But we've got to have a handshake agreement that you won't quit school when your eligibility's over.* So we shook hands on it. Chauncey played his fourth and final year, then returned the following year to complete his studies. He was working on a degree in Criminal Justice, and during his last year of school he got a lot more involved in our Criminal Justice Department. He helped arrange for a couple of guest speakers to come in and was really proactive in trying to help build that program.

A few months before he was scheduled to graduate, Chauncey planned to go home to Detroit for spring break. On his way there, he stopped to visit an uncle in Nashville. While they were preparing food for dinner, a fight between some teenagers broke out in the neighborhood. Chauncey, being a Criminal Justice major, went outside to break up the fight and told all of the teenagers to go home. About an hour later one of those teenagers came back with a gun and shot Chauncey to death in his uncle's house.

After Chauncey's funeral, I told our president about the agreement I had made with Chauncey. I knew how much that degree meant to Chauncey and how important it was to his family for him to be the first one to graduate from college. I told our President, *I promised Chauncey that he was going to get a degree from Martin Methodist College if he came back and studied. He held up his end of the bargain and I'd like us to do the same. Can we give him a degree posthumously?* He agreed and we decided to hold a special ceremony just for Chauncey's family at the start of the next school year.

We flew Chauncey's family in from Detroit. We had planned a genuine graduation ceremony for one person and all of our student-athletes were there. We had laid a cap and gown over a chair and when Chauncey's mom saw it she said, *I want to wear it. I want to wear Chauncey's gown and hat.* She put the cap and gown on and we had her walk across the stage to accept the diploma on Chauncey's behalf. She, her husband and their daughter were all crying as she did so and about half the crowd was in tears too. Everyone gave them a standing ovation.

It would have been easy to forget about that promise or to write the whole thing off, but giving that degree to Chauncey and his family was the right thing to do. It has been ten years since Chauncey was killed and we still stay in touch with Mrs. Shelton. When I spoke with her about a month ago, she told me, *Chauncey's sister is a senior in high school now. She wants to come down and look at Martin Methodist College where her brother graduated from.* That was such a cool thing to hear. Chauncey's little sister isn't sure this is where she wants to go, but as she does her college campus visits she wants to come look at Martin Methodist again through different eyes and perspective. To know that we were able to influence that young woman's life in a positive way despite the tragedy her family experienced was just an incredible feeling. Being able to do something unique like that for that young man and his family is my all-time number one collegiate experience.

SHAPING LIVES

• • • • • • •

MATT TANNEY
Director of Athletics
Western Illinois University

The intercollegiate athletic model in the United States is different from anywhere else in the world. We have an opportunity to shape 18- to 22-year-olds through both academics and athletics. There are so many different things they can learn through competing in high-level sports: how to deal with disappointment, how to persevere, how to bounce back from challenges, how to work together. When you take that and combine it with the opportunity to get a college degree, it's a powerful model that changes lives.

For a subset of our student-athletes, athletic ability is the driver that has created the opportunity for them to pursue a higher education. I'm really proud of the emphasis we've put on the educational component and the strides we've made in that area. It's heartbreaking when you see students who struggle academically but don't take advantage of the help and support we offer. I look at the students we serve and I think about the impact we'll have on them 20 years down the road. Did they have a good experience? Were we able to positively influence their lives? I think their overall experience can serve them well and prepare them for life much further down the road than just the next semester.

There have been a few instances where we've had student-athletes with undiscovered learning disabilities until their second or third year in the program. They're not getting work done at the rate they need to be and when we connect them to campus resources, it's something to the effect of: *Oh, you have dyslexia,* or *Oh, you have ADD,* or something else that has inhibited their academic ability throughout their life to that point. To me, that's more an indictment of flaws inherent in the secondary educational system than any individual student, and how students sometimes are unfairly pushed from level to level just to keep them moving. We've had more than one student-athlete in situations where we realize, *Had we known this or had this been addressed when you were a sophomore in high school, you would be in such a different place. BUT, we're glad you're here and we're glad we can address that because otherwise it never would have been addressed.* If not for the additional support from athletics, access to that help might not be available. Once we make those discoveries, we're able to help those student-athletes take steps to overcome their challenges. The one-on-one attention they receive as a byproduct of their participation in collegiate athletics makes such an incredible difference for them. Our staff is able to recognize a lot of those red flags and provide services that help them in a meaningful way.

Youth sports and sports at the high school level are important, but I strongly believe we have the most power to impact lives at the college level. The things 18- to 22-year-olds can learn when they're surrounded by good coaches and administrative staff will shape their lives and their futures unlike any other environment.

ACHIEVING POTENTIAL

• • • • • • •

BOBBY PURCELL

Executive Director of the Wolfpack Club and
Senior Associate Athletic Director
NC State University

Athletics creates a lot of opportunities for first generation college students, many of whom probably would not have gone to college otherwise. Our ability to offer scholarships to young athletes can change lives and families forever. I know some people believe that schools shouldn't recruit kids without good grades, but to me there's more to the decision than that. It's about seeing the character of a young man or young woman and being willing to take a chance on them. Being a bad student doesn't mean they're a bad kid; a lot of times, it just means they didn't have the resources or the parental support to achieve their potential academically.

Thinking back through my career, there are two young men who really stand out to me. I helped recruit both of them when I was on the NC State Football Staff in the early 1980's. Both young men were poor students but great character people.

The first young man was a top prospect. He had the physical size and skills to be a really good football player. Unfortunately, he was lacking from an academic standpoint. He had a speech impediment plus a little bit of a learning disability, and he came from a family that didn't have a lot of resources. His father was in prison and his mother was trying to raise four kids on a tenant farm by herself while working in a factory to make ends meet. They didn't have many books in their house; nobody read to him as a child and he didn't have anyone to help him with his homework growing up. The more we looked into this young man, the more we realized what a great, high-character individual he was. All the teachers loved him, the principal loved him, the guidance counselors loved him and his coaches loved him. They all gave him strong recommendations, so we took a chance on him and brought him to NC State. He was able to experience a lot of things that might not seem like a big deal to most people but which he'd never experienced before. He slept in an air-conditioned bedroom, he ate three meals a day, he flew on an airplane for the first time, and he met people of different races and different backgrounds. This young man worked his butt off in school. He hardly ever missed class; he was in study hall practically every night for five years. He did everything he was supposed to do but still struggled to make the grade. It wasn't a lack of effort, it was just his background. On the football field he excelled: he became a starter, played on TV and did television interviews, the whole thing. After five years of school, he had enough hours to graduate but he did not have a 2.0 GPA and just couldn't meet that requirement. He left NC State without a degree, but he had an education. He took a job on one of the university's research farms, so now he has health insurance and a retirement plan. He's probably the first in his family to have either of those things. He's married to a girl he met in college and their children are going to college. A lot of academic or media people might say we should have never signed that young man and that he wasn't qualified to go to college. But I'm more proud of him than anyone because he didn't have the advantages that other kids have. He's a total success story in my book.

The other young man we signed the same year had a similar story. Nobody in his family had ever graduated from high school, much less gone to college. They had a difficult home situation and he didn't have the resources to prepare for college. A lot of schools might have shied away from him because of his grades. But we took a chance on the young man because he was such a hard worker: he was captain of three sports teams, he never missed a day of school in 12 years, and he drove a school bus because back then you could do that in North Carolina as a high school junior and senior. He continued to work hard in college and was able to graduate from NC State, then go on to complete a Master's degree. He also married a college graduate.

Those are the kids I'm most proud of. Had it not been for athletics, neither of those young men would have had the opportunity to go to college. Even though only one of them graduated, both of them benefited from the education they received at NC State and that has changed their families forever. Young men and women like these have had to work harder than their peers because of the situations they were born into, and they've achieved more than some kids who had outstanding grades to start with. To me, creating those opportunities is the most powerful part of college athletics. I think we should celebrate those types of successes just as much as we celebrate the kids who make the Dean's List.

MAKING A DIFFERENCE

· · · · · · ·

TOM BOWEN
Athletic Director
University of Memphis

I grew up as the oldest of four sons in an Irish Catholic family, and I've always believed that God has a plan. I believed the plan for me was to go into the seminary. And I wanted to do that, but I also wanted to see what it would be like to play football at the next level.

After I graduated from Moreau Catholic High School, I went to the University of San Diego and participated in football my freshman year. It was exciting and fun, and I loved it! So after the season, I formally entered my studies for the priesthood with the congregation of the Holy Cross Fathers at the University of Notre Dame in 1980.

Initially, I believed my vocation was to become a Catholic priest who coached high school football. It seemed like the best of both worlds. I'd had the opportunity to meet Father Bill Seetch C.S.C., who was the head football coach at Notre Dame College Prep in Niles, Illinois at the time in 1980. Bill really inspired me to make a difference in the lives of young people through athletics, so I thought following in his footsteps was what I was being called to do.

I loved every day I spent in my religious formation and being in seminary. Religious life was a great experience for me. It taught me about servant leadership, which has helped me tenfold in my work in athletics. I eventually realized, though, that my calling had more to do with shaping the lives of young people through sports than with serving as a priest.

When I left the religious life in 1985, I became a religious studies teacher and head football coach at Saint Mary's High School in Colorado Springs. It was my first head coaching job, and I remember beating a school called Louis Palmer High School. We were the underdogs but we won 13-10. What an exhilarating moment! I thought then that my career would be coaching, because it was something I really enjoyed doing but God had other things in store for me.

After a couple of years in Colorado, I moved back to the San Francisco Bay area to work at De La Salle High School in Concord, California. A Christian Brother named Jerome Gallegos gave me the opportunity to serve as an athletic director of the school in 1987. That was when I started to delve into what it meant to be an athletic director. I quickly saw it was more far-reaching than just coaching or being part of one program. As an athletic director, I had the opportunity to guide the lives of every student. I realized that what we were doing in athletics - and football in particular - was making a difference in young people's lives.

When I became a Division I athletic director, that realization became very, very profound. You watch these students compete all year, you go to all the games, and then you're with them in May when their families are there to see them graduate with a college degree. That's the greatest moment.

There are people that we recruit and bring to our institution who never would have had a chance to go to college. If not for athletics, college wouldn't have happened for them: either they didn't have the money or they didn't have any opportunity or they didn't come from a family that focused on higher education. Many of these student-athletes are the first person in their entire family to go to college. No matter what their background or their story is, they earn a college degree and their life's forever changed. We help make that possible.

That's really, really cool, and that's why I've stayed in athletics. I've had numerous opportunities to go work at other levels, but I've stayed in college athletics because of the difference we make in the lives of our student-athletes. I look at all the kids we've worked with, and not everybody's going to play professionally, right? But everybody that we recruit can earn a college degree. They can change their future, and through athletics we are able to offer them that opportunity. I think our critics of our business sometimes forget how much that matters to families. That's a big deal and we have to remember that we're making a difference in the world that goes far beyond just winning or losing games.

UNLOCKING POTENTIAL

• • • • • • •

ROB MULLENS
Director of Athletics
University of Oregon

Everybody pays attention to what happens on TV: the results, the celebrations, maybe even some of the difficult defeats. But to me, the most meaningful thing we do isn't something that gets a lot of press. It's how athletic programs change the trajectory of young lives by giving student-athletes a chance they might never have had otherwise. After everything is said and done, graduation is the most important day of a student-athlete's career and our greatest reward is meeting the families of student-athletes and hearing their stories.

When somebody comes to a college athletic program, we're able to help them build their confidence and unlock their potential. We do more than simply train and coach athletes; we provide resources and a support system that can make a lifelong difference for somebody. In providing opportunity, we may have student-athletes arrive without the foundation of a "typical" college student. On occasion, these young men and women challenge the system or find themselves in difficult situations. We're there to give them guidance, provide the additional structure they need, maybe even give them a little tough love. Over the course of year two or three, you see them respond positively to the support system and thrive because they've caught up on those foundational elements. You get to watch as they begin to realize, *Wow, if I embrace this opportunity then I really can change my life and maybe even change my family's life.*

I've seen it happen at every program I've ever worked. I remember one time in particular, we had a women's golfer who came from a really difficult home life. Golf had given her an opportunity but she really struggled with the transition to the college environment. She was struggling to find her place: getting in trouble with alcohol, ignoring academic requirements, not doing the things she needed to do. We kept providing support services and looking for different ways to connect, but it was a difficult situation. Just as it reached the point where the coach had to consider removing her from the team, something finally clicked. After two years of struggle, you could see her turn the corner. So many times, young people like that are the ones who become leaders in their program or even team captains when they're fifth-year seniors. They become positive influences for other young people because they've seen what college can do for them and they want to give back in a similar way.

For me, some of the best moments have been hearing from former student-athletes that we were able to help. I remember getting a thank-you note from a football player who was a good student and took advantage of every opportunity we offered. He wrote, *I have two degrees from a great university and I don't have a dime in debt because of the support that you guys provided me.* And just a few weeks ago I got an email out of the blue from a former University of Oregon basketball player that said, *Thanks for everything that you did for me. I'm back in the area where I grew up and I'm just so appreciative of the opportunity I was given.*

That's one of the beauties of athletics: it provides access and opportunity for diverse populations and many first generation college students. Even though sometimes you might look at certain individuals on paper and think, *Wow, they may not fit at this institution, they may not have the foundation to succeed,* with the right kind of love and support you can help them realize their potential. That's powerful, and that's what makes what we do so worthwhile.

⑨
CHAPTER NINE
"COACH"

> **A coach is someone who tells you what you don't want to hear, and has you see what you don't want to see, so you can be who you have always known you can be.**
> *- Tom Landry*

Showing up to practice as a 6-year-old and seeing that my coach only had one arm was a bit startling to me all those years ago. I remember wondering how effective he could be with only one arm. But considering it was soccer, my logic wasn't quite fully formed on the subject. Coach Gene, as it was explained to me, had been involved in a work-related accident of some sort and ended up losing his arm just below the elbow. Sometimes he'd have a prosthetic hand and sometimes he'd have one of those hooks that you can control and grab stuff with. Most of the time though, it was just his arm. I have to admit, he could hold a surprising number of soccer balls under that arm and what I perceived to be a disability sure didn't seem to slow him down at all.

You'd think having only one arm would be enough to make a coach stand out in the memory of a child. But honestly, that's not what I remember most about Gene Owen. I remember that he was patient and kind and never seemed to get frustrated with us. I remember that he taught us all of the finer points about soccer and turned us into a really good team. I remember that of all the fathers of all of the kids, he was the one that volunteered to spend that time with us. I remember him as my first "Coach."

What is it about that word, "Coach," that is so powerful? I am fortunate to have been able to coach a few teams here and there, and the other day

I saw a kid who was on one of my son's little league teams. *Hey, Coach!* he exclaimed. I turned and saw that it was him, we exchanged hellos and how-ya-doings and went on about our days. I love being called "Coach." I loved it when I was coaching and I love to hear someone remember me as their coach years after the fact. It's silly, of course, that I get so much satisfaction out of that title. I mean, coaching is not my profession. I'm no Nick Saban and I realize that. But I take pride in being called "Coach" because I hope that someday these kids can look back and remember me as fondly as I remember Gene Owen. Because when I think of great coaches, that's who comes to mind.

I don't know if there's a single profession on earth that I respect more than the teaching profession. I respect it both because of the job they do and because it's something I could never do. Teachers are underpaid and overworked and we task them with far more than just educating our children. I don't just remember every coach I ever had. I can also name every teacher I had from Mrs. Frickenshmidt (yes, that was really her name) in kindergarten all the way through every teacher of every subject in high school. Unfortunately though, teachers don't get a cool title like "Coach." We call them Miss or Mrs. or Mr. and then whatever their last name is. Coaches get a title. And it's a coveted one.

John Wooden said, *If we, as coaches, aren't teachers, we are nothing.* And I think that sums up why the title of "Coach" is so special. It encapsulates so much. It means teacher. It means mentor. It means motivator and educator and friend. Combine that with the fact that they're teaching us and guiding us and mentoring us in sports, of all things, and you have something really exclusive.

I wanted to find out if other people agreed with me on this so we included a question in our fan survey about a coach's influence. It was important to know if fans, not people who make their living in sports, learned any life lessons from their coaches that remain with them years later. The response was as you'd anticipate: 97% of people said that yes, their coaches had impacted them in that way and 80% of people stated they still remember most or all of their coaches from when they played sports. Nearly half of them have turned around and coached in some capacity as a result of their own experiences playing sports and 86% of them felt like they were able to at least moderately shape the lives of those they coached.

Being a coach is an honor that should never be taken lightly. Coaches have the power to influence and guide young people in a way that almost no one else has. Coaches, like teachers, can empower youth to accomplish things they may never have thought they had the ability to accomplish. Nearly everyone I spoke with for this book made reference to the impact one or more of their coaches had in their lives. Honestly, this entire book could have probably been about coaches and their effect on student-athletes because every story somehow seems to relate to that. That speaks to just how influential a coach can be.

My grandmother passed away a few years ago and when I arrived at her funeral, a familiar face walked up to me to say hello. It took me a bit to recognize him but after a moment, I realized who it was. Coach Gene, believe it or not, was the chaplain tasked with officiating that summer afternoon's graveside service. I had no idea that he'd gone into the ministry but it was no surprise that he wanted to spend a life serving others. That's what coaches do.

COACH McGRAW

• • • • • • •

BARRY ALVAREZ
Director of Athletics
University of Wisconsin

I grew up in a small mining town in Pennsylvania. My high school class only had about 120 people in it, but we had a very good youth football program. The community was very supportive of athletics and the coaches were all very dedicated to the program. That provided the kids with a very solid foundation.

I had a tough, old Irish coach named Pat McGraw that coached me in every sport I played: football, basketball and baseball. I was even his bat boy in his summer baseball leagues. In preparation for the football season, the league allowed each team to have two preseason scrimmages against other teams. Coach McGraw would schedule us to scrimmage the biggest schools he could get so we'd be going against the toughest competition out there. Here you had this small town team, barely more than 30 guys, loading onto a school bus, and to add to that, we looked like a bunch of raga-muffins. Our jerseys were old sweatshirts with three-quarter length sleeves with no numbers on them. Our pants were these old things we'd just rinse out after practice and hang up on the fence around the field to dry. We were a sight to behold.

So here we were, a Double-A school driving up to these Quad-A schools that not only had a lot more kids but also a lot more money. We'd pile off the bus in our practice uniforms and see a hundred guys run out of their locker room in their fancy game uniforms, circling the field and doing calisthenics. Our eyes were as big as baseballs. They had three times as many guys and they were dressed to the nines. Coach McGraw must have realized they had a mental edge on us after seeing us standing there staring at them with our mouths wide open. Coach always had this big wad of chew in his mouth, so here's our coach and he gathers us up, spits the chew and says, *Let me just tell you something. I don't care what they wear and I don't care how many they have. They can only put 11 on the field. And our 11 will kick their 11's ass.*

And that's exactly what happened.

That taught me a lesson that I've carried with me my entire life. Years later when I was inducted into the College Football Hall of Fame, a reporter asked me, *Does it surprise you that you come from a small town and were able to attain this honor?* And I said, *No. I had great coaching from the time I started playing football as a little kid. I played for a great coach, Hall of Famer Bob Devaney. I coached with Hayden Fry and Lou Holtz, two other Hall of Famers. And I always felt like the sky was the limit for me regardless of where I was from.*

It all goes back to that speech from Coach McGraw. He taught me that I could achieve anything. And when I arrived at Wisconsin, I had to put that same idea into our players' heads. Regardless if we're playing teams like Ohio State or Michigan with all of their history and success and great recruiting classes, none of that matters. They can only put 11 men on the field – same as us. And our 11 are going to kick their 11's ass. That's the attitude my teams always had.

COACH SMITH

• • • • • • •

MICHAEL BEALE
Assistant Athletic Director for Marketing
University of North Carolina

The 2009-2010 season marked the 100th anniversary of Carolina Basketball, so about a year and a half out we started planning a big event. We knew this was going to be a once-in-a-lifetime experience for a lot of folks and we wanted to make it really special.

Coach Smith coached at Carolina for 36 years from 1961-1997 and is widely regarded as a coaching legend. We started talking to former players, coaches, and managers about coming back for the 100 Years of Carolina Basketball celebration and when one of them mentioned they might not be able to make it, we'd tell them that Coach Smith was going to be involved in it and he would love for them to be there. Their answers quickly became *Alright, if Coach Smith wants me there, then I'll be there.* Seeing the influence that Coach Smith still had on all of these people and how he could still move them to do things - it was awesome.

Without anyone really intending it to happen, our gala to honor the 100 Years of Carolina Basketball quickly became a gala to honor Coach Smith. That's the furthest thing in the world from what he ever would have wanted, but it was the number one desire of his former coaches, players and managers. I think a lot of us realized that this was probably going to be one of the last times we saw Coach Smith publicly because his health was beginning to decline. We knew he wouldn't want to be the focal point of the evening, so we worked closely with his family to keep everything a secret from him. I can't even remember exactly how we got him there that day but we did it.

The stands at the Smith Center were packed the night of the gala and we had a star-studded group of several hundred former players and managers on the court. We lowered the lights and played a tribute video that our video guys and a local historian had put together. The video was everyone's chance to say thank you to Coach Smith for everything he had done, and it was one of the most moving tributes I have ever seen. A lot of the stories people told weren't even related to basketball, they were just about what Coach Smith meant to them as a person and how he had helped shape their lives. A lot of people talked about how they still make decisions based on what Coach Smith had taught them. It really summed up everything he stood for as a coach and as a human being. I don't think there was a dry eye in the entire place when the video ended.

As we brought the lights back up, we walked Coach Smith out of the tunnel and onto the court. I've been involved in some unbelievable basketball games here, but I've never heard it louder than it was in that moment. Coach Smith sheepishly acknowledged the crowd and in his usual, kind way he asked everybody to please sit and quiet down. I think that might have been the first time those players had ever disregarded something he was telling them to do. This was their chance to say thank you to a man who never wanted to be thanked for anything and they weren't going to give up that opportunity. Every single player there came up to shake Coach Smith's hand or hug him. There were several former NBA players there and as they came forward, Coach Smith would kind of step away and show his hands toward the player to encourage the crowd to recognize that person, but no one was having it. For everyone there, this was a night that was all about honoring Coach Smith. His impact on the basketball players had been profound but his presence and influence had extended far beyond his players and had touched many people outside of basketball. As you looked around that night you could see people in the stands sobbing, just overcome with emotion. That night was the last real opportunity for the public and Carolina Basketball to say, *Thank you, Coach Smith. Thank you for everything you've done for this basketball program and this university and this community.* It was one of the most powerful moments I've ever witnessed.

There are plenty of wins on and off the court, plenty of highlights and lowlights, but it's moments like this that I know I'll never get to experience again. That night is something I'll carry with me for the rest of my life. Moments like that are why I do what I do.

GIVING BACK

· · · · · · ·

BRIAN WICKSTROM
Director of Athletics
University of Louisiana – Monroe

In this business, I've met so many great people who are former stu-dent-athletes. I think that's what college athletics does: it breeds fantastic people who've had a great experience and want to share that with others.

As a high school all-American in the 400-meters, I had a lot of college options to choose from. After visiting several different schools, I decided to stay in-state and chose Kansas State University. I had grown up being more of a Kansas fan, but K-State actually flew me and my twin brother to Man-hattan, Kansas on a little plane for our official visit. We were so impressed. They made us feel like we were really important.

When I got to Kansas State, I thought I was all-world. In high school I had been a stand-out, but in college I turned out to be just another guy. The track team was so good that there were a lot of weeks I didn't race or make the travel squad. That could have been a really rude awakening, but the track coach and the athletic director were such great people and so sup-portive that it didn't matter. I didn't mind being an average guy because the coaches cared so genuinely about each of us. It was enough just to be there and be a part of this incredible family they'd created. All of my best college memories involve hanging out with my teammates and other student-ath-letes at K-State.

I vividly remember a conversation I had with Daryl Anderson, the sprint coach, during my junior year when he was giving me a ride over to the outdoor track. I had been thinking about my future, and I told him: *You know what? I really wish I could be an athletic director.* I didn't know much about the various jobs in the industry, I just knew that it was something I wanted to stay involved with because I'd had such a great experience. Daryl said to me, *You've accomplished a lot in your life. You can do anything you set your mind to. Set your mind to it and you can become an athletic director someday.*

So I set my mind to it by applying for jobs, internships and even volunteer internships during my senior year. Unfortunately, I was just another guy in that competitive environment too. I couldn't get a single interview. I stayed at Kansas State for a fifth year and completed my MBA, certain that would help me get where I wanted to go, but the same thing happened: no interviews. My dad told me it was time to get a job one way or the other, so when I graduated I took a job in banking.

After spending some time working for a big Midwestern regional bank, I was hired to help build up and sell a community bank. I was making really good money - $86,000 a year back in 1998 – but I hated banking. I remember sitting at the table after we had closed on the sale of the community bank, which had generated four-and-a-half times the book value for the owners. My team was energized by how successful we'd been and they were talking about moving to Palm Springs to do the same thing for another bank, but I just couldn't get excited about it. That was a pivotal moment for me. I remember thinking, *Man, I know they made a lot of money but... this isn't what I want to do with my life.*

I decided to quit my job and get a Masters in Sports Administration at Ohio University. It was a huge change to go from being a guy who made a lot of money to being a guy who barely had enough to get by. Instead of flying around the country and taking trips whenever I wanted, I was driving an old, paid-off 1984 Ford Escort GT. I was going to school and teaching seven classes and earning just $740 a month before taxes, but I was happier than I had been in years.

My first job after graduation was working as a Development Associate at the University of Missouri. The starting salary was only a thousand dollars a month plus benefits, although after about six months they brought it up to $24,000 per year. It was a fraction of what I had been making before, but that didn't matter to me. What mattered was how I felt about the work

I was doing and the people I got to work with. Laird Veatch and Ross Bjork still stand out as two of the best bosses I've ever had. While I was there, I also had the opportunity to meet Joe Parker, who later helped me make the transition from Associate AD at Santa Clara University to Assistant Athletic Director at University of Michigan. Joe's one of the best people I've ever met in my life. Laird, Ross and Joe had been student-athletes themselves and are just genuinely great human beings. People like that are what makes others want to be part of this profession.

This industry is often thankless. You work ridiculous hours, you scratch and claw and make very little money for the first several years that you do it. It's insane! If you advertised a job with that type of description, most people would walk away. The people who work in this business do it because they have a passion for it. Like me, many are former student-athletes who had the opportunity to make lifelong friendships and learn from great mentors while competing in a sport that they love. They know the power and impact that collegiate athletics can have. My experience at Kansas State makes me want to give back to every student-athlete I can, so they can have the type of experience that I had. That's why I'm in this business.

TRIBUTE TO A COACH

• • • • • • •

JEN COHEN
Director of Athletics
University of Washington

In 2015, the University of Washington played its season opener at Boise State. It was Chris Petersen's second year as our head football coach. Before Chris came to us, he had spent eight seasons at Boise State where he accumulated a 92-12 record and was a two-time Bear Bryant Award winner. We had planned the game at Boise State prior to hiring him, so the game was something he kind of inherited. Chris is a pretty private guy, but I think we all knew there were some strong emotions involved in him going back to Boise State as the coach for another team. It's a tough thing to do. Boise State was a place that had given him so much; it's a place where he had raised his family and to which he had dedicated a large part of his life.

When we got to Boise, we had the traditional police escort coming into the stadium. As we rounded the corner of the stadium, I noticed all these people lined up on both sides of the street. At first, I thought, *Oh, this must be something they do when their team comes in and that's cool. Lots of schools have different traditions like that.* Then I realized they were all lining the path of the buses in order to see Chris Petersen. There were hundreds of people holding signs about how much they loved him, with pictures of him and slogans and things like *Thank you, Thank you.*

The crowd kept going as we drove one half of the stadium length. There must have been thousands of people! Seeing all those people waving appreciation signs and calling out to Chris was unbelievable. When we got to the front of the stadium to drop our guys off, there was a huge crowd of Boise State fans waiting for Chris like a welcome party. It was their moment to show appreciation to a coach they had loved and hadn't really had the chance to say goodbye to when the coaching change happened. I was glad I had my sunglasses on because seeing their love for him made me extremely emotional. When I looked around, a couple of staff members who were sitting in the front of the bus with me were welling up, too. I was just like, *Damn, have you ever seen anything like this?* None of us had. The whole game was like that: Boise State fans finding ways to show Chris their respect and appreciation. When he came out of the tunnel on the opposing side, they gave him a standing ovation. When the game was over, all these people waited around to cheer for him again. It was an epic tribute and I can't even imagine what Chris was feeling.

In that moment I think we realized how special he was and how lucky we were to have him. Seeing the impact one guy could have on an entire university and an entire community was such a great example of how beautiful sports can be. You could just feel how much he meant to that entire town. I think they respected not only the wins he had brought them but also what a quality person he is and what he does for student-athletes. Chris is a guy who puts his kids first; he has a high standard of what he thinks they can achieve in their lives and he's the last one to run out of the tunnel behind them. When somebody's as consistent as he was with those principles over a period of time, it's just magical. Chris re-inspired all of us here to believe that we could compete at the highest levels and still do it the right way: with values and principles and a deep care for the kids and for our community.

I think the reason that experience was so powerful to me is not just because of what it said about Chris Petersen, but what it said about the Boise State fans. It's unprecedented for an opposing team to come out and support a former coach like that. We still talk about it here all the time: *Craziest thing we've ever seen; best sportsmanship I've ever seen in college sport; never seen anything like it; we'll always be a Boise State fan now because of the way those fans embraced him and showed their appreciation for him.* Fans are an extension of your overall brand and they have a tremendous influence on the gameday experience and the game itself. That's a big part of why different teams have different reputations. The way those Boise State fans paid tribute to a coach they had loved and respected spoke volumes about their program and their community.

COACH SUTTON

• • • • • • •

WREN BAKER
Vice President and Director of Athletics
University of North Texas

During my junior year at Southeastern University, I was in the honors program. One of our responsibilities was to pair up with a faculty member and interview four high school candidates who wanted to be in the honors program too. I can't remember the name of the faculty member I was paired with, but I remember him asking a young lady we were interviewing, *What are you going to major in? Do you know what you want to be?* She kind of leaned forward and started talking about how she would love to be a teacher because the thought of helping kids grow and develop really intrigued her, but she wasn't going to major in education because there was no money in it. This faculty member told her, *With the way that you lit up and the energy that came to you when you talked about being a teacher, you're making a huge mistake if you don't major in education. You need to do what you're passionate about.*

I couldn't get that conversation out of my mind. I was majoring in computer science and after that interview I couldn't stop thinking, *Am I going to sit behind a computer all day, is that what my life's going to be? Will that be rewarding?* The previous summer I had interned at the Weyerhaeuser Paper Mill back home in Valliant, OK where my whole family worked and I had quickly figured out that wasn't for me. I remember hearing one of my bosses say, *Hey, you keep doing a good job, get your degree, and we may offer you a job here!* and just thinking, *Oh my God, I never want to do that.*

Between that experience at the paper mill and the comments that faculty member made, the question of what I was going to do with my life was weighing heavy on my heart. I spent a lot of time thinking about it and praying about it. That same semester I had taken a course for fun called "Theories of Coaching Basketball" because I had always enjoyed sports as a kid. The course was taught by the head men's basketball coach, and one day after class was over he said to me, *I think you've got a gift for understanding kids and understanding motivation. Would you want to be a student assistant coach?* And for me that was just confirmation of where I was being led. The best thing I can compare it to is almost like a Jerry McGuire moment, where I looked at the path I had been on and was like, *You know what? I'm not doing this.* I quit the job I'd had in the computer lab, changed majors without even talking to my parents, and started working for free for the men's basketball program. It was awesome. I started to really understand what that faculty member had meant about passion because I had finally found mine.

As I was graduating and looking for a job, I went through the College Blue Book and wrote letters to every men and women's basketball program that I would ever conceivably work for. To give my letters a higher chance of being seen by a coach I even overnighted the ones that were in-state, which at the time seemed like it cost a fortune. I got a letter back from Coach Sutton that said, *We don't have anything available but if you come to Oklahoma State you're welcome to come by practice. I'd love to meet you.* That was really exciting because I was a huge Eddie Sutton fan. I had grown up watching him coach Oklahoma State basketball back when even just getting to see a game on TV was a really big deal. I hadn't planned to drive to Stillwater but I wasn't going to pass up the opportunity to meet him, so I called his office and said, *I got this letter from Coach Sutton and he said if I was going to come to Oklahoma State to come by and introduce myself. I'm going to be on campus in a few days. Can I come by?* They got back with me and said yes, so I went.

When I got to his office, Coach Sutton came walking out and I'll never forget this: he was eating popcorn. He said, *Hey can you wait a few minutes? I want a couple of guys to sit in with us.* And I thought, *well that's odd.* I wasn't dressed up for an interview or anything, I was just wearing slacks and a polo shirt. The other people came in and he asked me a few questions, then said, *I've got a Graduate Assistant spot that's opened up and I'm committed to talk to a couple of other people but I'm real interested in you. Would you have an interest?* And I'm like, *Are you kidding me?! Yeah!* A few days later he called me and asked if I'd come back up to visit with the rest of the staff, so I did. Then he offered me the job. That was a huge moment of affirmation that I'd made the right choice. There were literally tens of thousands, if not hundreds of thousands of people, who would have liked to have that opportunity, and it just kind of happened for me. It was pretty amazing.

Working for Coach Sutton was awesome. He taught me so much about work ethic and what it takes to be good at what you do. He was an incredible mentor, and he helped me understand that *I want to be X* means nothing if you're not willing to pay the price and go through the process to achieve it every single day.

I spent four years there, two as a graduate assistant and two as full-time basketball operations assistant, then an opportunity came up for me to return to my hometown and be the Athletic Director and Principal at Valliant Public Schools. I was reluctant to leave college athletics behind but it seemed like the right decision at the time because I was getting married, I needed more money, it was in my hometown and it was only an hour from my wife's hometown. Coach Sutton and I talked about it several times and he understood what was driving my decision. He knew I felt like it was best for my wife and my family even though it wasn't really what I wanted to do. But when I went in there to tell him, *Coach I'm going to take the job,* he was like, *Why would you do that?! This is the dumbest decision a smart guy's ever made. You'll never get back into college athletics.*

Seven or eight months later he played an integral role in helping me do just that. In December, I got a call from the President of Rogers State University and he said, *Hey, my name is Joe Wiley, I'm the President at Rogers State University, the fastest-growing university in Oklahoma. I'm starting athletics and I need a young up-and-coming AD who can also coach basketball because I don't have a lot of money. I've talked to four people and three of them gave me your name.* Coach Sutton was one of those three people. It was like he knew where I needed to be. For the second time in my career, he made it possible for me to do what I love to do.

This business can be tough. There's no clear career progression and no straightforward recipe for success; so much depends on catching a break and just knowing people. I've been fortunate to experience a lot of moments that reaffirmed I was on the right path and I've had the opportunity to learn from amazing people like Coach Sutton. I know there's no way that I would be where I am today if this wasn't the plan God had for me.

A COACH'S IMPACT

• • • • • • •

PETER ROBY
Director of Athletics & Recreation
Northeastern University

There's almost no other relationship like the one that forms between a coach and a player. The amount of time you spend with each other, the emotion involved and invested in it, the near-constant feedback loop, the trust and respect that's required both ways and the opportunity to experience such highs and the lows together... all of that can form a powerful bond that lasts a lifetime. It can be an experience that positively affects the player throughout their entire life.

The opposite is true, too. Having a negative experience between coach and player can set people back and leave a bad taste in their mouth. If that happens, they don't stay connected, they don't give back and they don't want to support the program they attended.

The way I was treated as an athlete growing up led me to promise myself that if I ever got the opportunity to influence young people through sports, I would make it as positive as possible. It has inspired me to try to create the kind of environment that helps kids thrive and achieve their goals.

Much of my own social, educational and personal growth took place through athletics. I started playing sports at a young age and my father was there for me every step of the way, from my Little League days to practicing on the asphalt in my hometown to driving long distances for high school games. As we'd drive to and from games, or sit at a restaurant having ice cream after a game, my father would talk with me about life and about being a good person. He taught me a lot of valuable lessons, and all of it was surrounded in the context of a sport.

In college, I had a coach named Gary Walters. He was a tough guy to play for. He demanded the most from you, but he did it in a way that made you better. It really made you appreciate your teammates and the experience. Oftentimes, we would sit on the court before or after practice and have discussions about who you are as a person, what kind of role you're playing and how all those things can manifest themselves on the basketball court. He pushed you to be the best you could be - not only as an athlete but as a student and as a person. That stuck with me, because it was very consistent with what my father did as I was growing up.

Both my dad and Coach Walters taught me that it's not just about whether you score the points or touchdowns in the game, but also what kind of teammate you are. How are you motivating your teammates? What kind of effort are you putting forth every day? Are you challenging yourself and making the competition greater in practice so that the games themselves are easier? And what kind of lessons are you learning about resilience and perseverance and humility and leadership and toughness?

Recently, we had an event at Northeastern University for our basketball alumni and current players. One of our guys got up and spoke about the bond he felt between the coaching staff and his fellow players. He talked about how all his teammates still care deeply about the program even to this day and stay in touch with each other. Then he compared that to the guys that he was playing with professionally overseas. He talked about how they had no relationship with their coach or their teammates and because of that, it just wasn't a very positive experience. He said that the thing that made the greatest difference at Northeastern was the environment and how we treated one another. Knowing you helped make a positive difference in one's life is a powerful thing to hear from one of your former players.

When you've had a great experience in sports, it's something that makes you say to yourself, *If that was that valuable to me, wouldn't it be great if I could have the same type of impact on others?* It's something that inspires you to give back and make a difference. And when you serve as the right kind of role model for others, they'll want to pay it forward too.

JACK BRUEN

· · · · · · ·

MARK MURPHY
President
Green Bay Packers

When I was named Athletic Director at Colgate in 1992, Jack Bruen was our head basketball coach. Colgate has a lot of strong tradition in football and hockey but very little basketball tradition. We'd never been in the NCAA Basketball Tournament or anything like that. Jack had a long and successful coaching history and we hoped he would be able to help us build a stronger program.

Around the same time that we hired Jack, we recruited a player named Adonal Foyle who was one of the top recruits in the country. He chose Colgate over Duke and Syracuse. Having Jack and Adonal really put Colgate on the map from a basketball perspective. During Adonal's freshman and sophomore years, we made it to the NCAA Tournament and won the Patriot League. It was a really exciting time. For Jack, it was both the best of times and the worst of times. We were having unprecedented success but there was a lot of pressure to keep winning, and the situation with Adonal was complicated because his guardians were Colgate professors. During Adonal's junior year we had a little bit of a downturn in our performance and he left the program early to go pro as a lottery pick in the NBA.

That summer, Jack wasn't feeling too great but we didn't know what was wrong with him. I remember playing in a golf tournament with him and he couldn't really take full swings with the golf club. Then in September, he was diagnosed with pancreatic cancer. Jack wanted to continue coaching and as an Athletic Director, I remember wondering, *Is it really right to allow him to coach? Is that the best thing for him?* We talked it through with Jack and our team physician to ensure we weren't putting him at any extra risk by letting him coach. At the end of the day it was what he loved to do; to take that away would have been cruel when he was already facing an incredibly difficult situation.

Every year, Colgate plays Syracuse in the Carrier Dome in the early part of the season. We've probably lost that game to Syracuse for 50 years in a row. When Adonal was with the program we all thought, *This might be our chance to beat Syracuse!* All three of those years, Syracuse just killed us. The year after Adonal left, Jack was weak and thin by the time we got to the Carrier Dome game. Jim Boeheim, the Syracuse coach, said that seeing Jack on the other bench like that made it one of the most difficult games he'd ever coached. Our players wanted to win that game so badly for Jack and they gave it everything they had. Watching the team play above itself for his sake was one of the most amazing things I've ever seen. The game ended up coming right down to the wire and we lost, but seeing those players pour their hearts out on the court for Jack was unbelievable. I've never been more proud of a group of athletes in my life.

Jack ended up dying in late December. It was a difficult loss for all of us, especially the team. To me, the way those players rose above themselves to support Jack epitomizes the type of character that's built through athletics. Athletics offers a lot of life lessons and the better the coach the more powerful those lessons can be. You learn that it isn't all about winning and you learn how to stick together as a team. You also learn how to handle defeat; how to come back from something difficult, learn from it and use it to motivate you to become better. Some coaches look at their situation and say, *Oh my gosh, I could never win now.* The better coaches say, *How can I learn from this? How can we benefit from it?* And the best coaches, like Jack, inspire those around them to respond positively to even the greatest challenges.

COACH MATERNE

• • • • • • •

WARDE MANUEL
Athletic Director
University of Michigan

When I was a student at Brother Martin High School in New Orleans, I had a football coach named Mike Materne. During my sophomore year it seemed like no matter what I did, Coach Materne would always yell at me. I was a pretty big kid and I was a starter, so I'm sure I was making plenty of mistakes. But it seemed like when other guys would do things or make mistakes that were bigger than mine, Coach wouldn't yell at them with the same level of intensity.

One day at practice, Coach was yelling at me as usual and I just got really mad. I couldn't take it any more and I walked away from him. I was so upset that I got tears in my eyes. Coach kept yelling at me but I didn't turn around. I just kept walking away from him, ignoring him as he called my name. Finally, he ran and caught up with me. When we were face to face and he could see the tears in my eyes, he yelled at me again: *What's your problem?!*

I told him, *Every time I do something wrong, no matter how small, you yell at me. But you don't yell at the other guys that much.* And I'll never forget what Coach Materne told me. He said, *Warde, you have more potential than the other guys. What I want to do is help you reach your greatest potential. That's why I'm hard on you. If I stop yelling at you, if I stop talking to you, that's the day I stop caring about how well you do.*

Having Coach explain that to me was really important and it shaped my view of things so much. From that point on, I started to look at feedback in a different way. Instead of seeing it as somebody trying to tear me down, I started to think of it as somebody trying to help me improve and succeed, no matter how that feedback was delivered. When I went on to play football at the University of Michigan, having that perspective was really important.

That lesson has stayed with me my entire life. As a player, you have a healthy combination of respect and fear when it comes to your coach. But a lot of times you don't realize why they do things or just how much they're teaching you. Every coach I've ever known talks to their players about more than simply succeeding at a sport; they talk about what it takes to succeed as a person. It's a different type of learning than being in a classroom and it shapes you in ways a classroom experience never could. Many of the qualities athletics teaches are important qualities for the rest of your life. Because of my experiences as a student-athlete, I feel prepared to handle the stress and the competition that exists in the world.

I believe that we're obligated to help the young people in our program not only become their best athletically but also guide them in becoming better prepared to succeed in all the other aspects of their lives. They deserve our feedback because they deserve the opportunity to reach their greatest potential.

⑩
CHAPTER TEN
WE ARE LEGION

> "Football fans share a universal language that cuts across many cultures and many personality types. A serious football fan is never alone. We are legion, and football is often the only thing we have in common."
>
> *- Hunter S. Thompson*

In the summer of 2004, I took my first trip to Chapel Hill, NC. I had recently started Old Hat and Rick Hart, my old jogging buddy and the current Director of Athletics at SMU, did me the favor of calling UNC on my behalf to see if they might have some work for me. Fortunately, they did and we've been working with UNC ever since. I made my way out there to discuss the details of what we'd be doing for the Tar Heels, and afterward I went over to the nearest apparel shop to grab a souvenir or two. I picked up a navy blue Nike hoodie that had the word "CAROLINA" embroidered across the front of it and more than a dozen years later I'm still wearing that thing as often as I get the chance.

On a recent trip to Charleston, SC, I happened to be wearing that very sweatshirt as I went to get my wife some yogurt from the market down the street. A fella was walking my direction and as he got closer he pointed at me and said in a louder-than-expected voice, *Go Heels!* Now, I'll be honest. I was a bit startled and it took me a minute to figure out what he said and why he said it to *me*, specifically. I had to remind myself that I was wearing a UNC sweatshirt. Fortunately I was able to gather my thoughts quickly enough to offer a stuttered, *Yeah! Go Heels!* back at him before my confusion became too obvious. It was good preparation for an encounter I had no more than two minutes later when I was actually in the market and another man gave me a hearty, *Go Heels!* I was more prepared this time and was quicker with my response.

Believe it or not, the point of this chapter is not to talk about my wardrobe or my interactions at the corner market. It's to talk about the bonds we form as fans. Hunter S. Thompson's quote references football fans specifically but the idea applies to any fan of any sport. We share a universal language that cuts across many cultures and many personality types. We are never alone. We are legion and sports is often the only thing we have in common.

When was the last time you were wearing your favorite Aerosmith t-shirt and some stranger yelled, *Sweet Emotion!* at you? Or the last time you were wearing that old Incredible Hulk t-shirt and passed a guy that gave you a hearty, *RAAARRRRRRR!!!!!* No, sports fans are in a justice league of their own. And for some reason, though startling, we don't question it when a random person yells, *Go X!* at us in the restroom at the bar across from Xavier's campus when he sees that we're wearing a Musketeers shirt.

Sports creates a bond between people who would otherwise be complete strangers and gives them something to connect over. Just like that Arkansas fan I met on the airplane. We didn't even share the same team in common. Our bond was formed over the fact that I'm a Sooner fan, Barry Switzer used to coach the Sooners, Barry Switzer played at Arkansas and the guy from the plane is an Arkansas fan. We connected over a former coach of my team that is a former player from his team. Sports fans are just searching for something that unites them!

The camaraderie between sports fans is obvious. I'm not uncovering any brilliant revelation here. But I did want to see how many sports fans recognize it themselves. In our fan survey, we asked how many of the participants felt a sense of camaraderie with people at sporting events. We further clarified the question by adding that they should not include people they were attending with. In other words, to what extent do you feel connected with all of the people at those events that you don't even know? Seventy-five percent of them said that they feel "a lot" and/or "a great deal" of connection with all those strangers with whom, beyond wearing the same color and cheering for the same team, they share no known commonalities.

Isn't that kinda nuts? Seventy-five percent of sports fans feel a connection with people they don't even know, for one reason and one reason only: they're all staring at the same rectangle and want the group of people in red to score more points than the group of people in blue.

Like I said, the connection between sports fans isn't breaking news. Every sports fan has experienced it. What you may not have realized, however, is the positive effect sports fans can have on an athletics program. The ever-important home field advantage is because of fans. Those scholarships that we talked about in Chapter 8 wouldn't exist without the fans. And as you'll see through some of the stories in this section, fans can affect an athletic program in ways we probably never would have considered. Eighty percent of those polled think that fans can either "probably" or "definitely" affect the outcome of the game. But there's no doubt in *my* mind that through the many contributions they make, fans have a huge impact on wins and losses.

If you take one thing away from this chapter, let it be this: Sports does not happen without every member of the team working toward achieving success. It does not happen without the athletes. It does not happen without the coaches. And it sure as hell doesn't happen without the fans. If you are a sports fan, take pride in what you give to the game. If you are an athlete, thank the fans for wanting to watch you play. If you are a coach, try to tune out the criticism of those people that think you should have gone for it on 4th-and-27 from your own 12-yard-line instead of punting, and relish the opportunity you have to affect the lives of young people through your job.

TOMMY SAPPINGTON

• • • • • • •

ROSS BJORK
Vice Chancellor for Intercollegiate Athletics
University of Mississippi

There's a guy who lives 30 miles away from campus. His name is Tommy Sappington, and he owns a clothing store. Tommy graduated from Ole Miss in 1978.

I met Tommy when I getting ready to speak at an alumni event in New Albany, Mississippi. We were 15 minutes early for the event and when we pulled up on Main Street, the Sappington's store was right in front of us. So we decided to stop in for five minutes just to see what they had. It was a cool store. They had suits and women's clothing and all kinds of Ole Miss stuff. There weren't any other customers at the time, and this guy came up and offered to help us. We told him we were just looking around and started talking about the Ole Miss gear. The guy looks at me and he's like, *Hey, aren't you - aren't you the Athletic Director at Ole Miss?* I introduced myself and he introduced himself as Tommy Sappington.

We started talking about how he loves having Ole Miss gear in the store and how he enjoys talking to the people who come in to buy it for game weekends. Tommy told me he was a graduate and a big fan. Since it was August and football season was just around the corner, I asked him where he normally sits at the games. Tommy looked at me and said, *Oh, I've never been to a game.*

My jaw hit the floor. I was like, *You've got to be kidding me. Wait a second: you live 30 miles away, you say you're a big fan, you're an alumnus.*

What do you mean you've never been to a game? How is that possible? You know, anybody who lives in Mississippi who's an Ole Miss fan has been to a football game at least once.

Well, he said, *my dad opened this store when I was seven years old and I started working for him when I was seven years old. We're open on Saturdays. It's my wife and I who run the store now, so we can't leave the store on Saturdays. We can't go to a game.* I just looked at him and thought, *Wow, that's dedication. Here's a man who's a big fan but can't go to games because he has to run his business, and he's doing everything he can to support and promote the program his own way.* Right then and there, I decided I'd make sure Tommy got to experience a game at least once. So I told him that I was going to help him get to a game. And he's like, *No, I can't leave the store, it's not going to work.* I told him, *You will come to the football game as my guest. I'm going to make sure it happens. We'll take care of you.*

I went to my alumni event and told the story to the crowd. They all knew Mr. Sappington and how he won't leave the store, even for a game. So I asked them, *Who can help me get Tommy to the football game? Surely somebody can watch the store.* They all looked at me like I was crazy. *Not going to happen,* they said. *He's so dedicated, he's kind of stubborn, he's just not going to leave the store on Saturdays. That's a big day for him.*

When I got back to the office the next day, I wrote Tommy a personalized note inviting him to a game. I included the football schedule and said, *Pick your game. You're my guest.* And sure enough, he took me up on it. He came to the Alabama game - the biggest game of the year.

What was so cool is that his son-in-law wrote me a letter soon after that thanking me for the invitation. He said, *We have tried for my entire adult life to get Tommy to come to a game and he never would. He probably wouldn't ever have done it except for your invitation. Thank you for making it personal. Thank you for thinking of us and reaching out.*

I don't care how much guys like Tommy Sappington can give to the program, I want them to be part of it in whatever way they can. Tommy's way of giving was to carry as much Ole Miss gear in his store as possible and share his enthusiasm for the program with his customers. He couldn't give financially and he couldn't go to the games, but he was committed to helping promote Ole Miss in other ways. That's the power of athletics inspiring people to do their part. I often tell that story when I speak to people about giving and being involved. I say, *Hey, look, it doesn't matter if it's giving $5, carrying t-shirts in your store, or donating $5 million. The point is, just give what you can because you love the university.*

WHAT IT IS REALLY ALL ABOUT

• • • • • • •

CRAIG PINTENS
Senior Associate Athletic Director
University of Oregon

Early in my career, I worked at University of Texas – Pan American. At the time, it was a Division I independent, located in Edinburg, Texas, near the Mexican border. We did not really have a marketing staff, just a hired student and me and sometimes, if we were lucky, a volunteer.

In my second year at UTPA, we had a home basketball game against Air Force in February. Like all of our games it was non-conference, but this one was a big deal because Air Force was ranked number 27 (we realize there is only a top 25, but Air Force was in *others receiving votes*) and was destined for the NCAA tournament, which they ended up making. We wanted to get a good turnout, so we plastered campus with everything imaginable to advertise the game: handbills, posters, handouts, anything we could think of. We probably broke a bunch of guidelines for the university but we wanted to make sure we got the word out. We ended up with over 3,500 people there, which was the biggest crowd we had in the two years I was at UTPA. We probably had 20 students in the stands, which certainly does not qualify as large, but it was about 16 more than predicted based on our previous games.

It was a tight game, but midway through the second half, we were winning. It was a great atmosphere, despite the minuscule student turnout. I wanted to thank the students who came out to the game, but that was a challenge because we did not have a student section and they were scattered throughout the gym. In addition, I was in charge of our game management, seated next to the occasionally freelancing P.A. announcer, making sure the band - which was six people - was playing at the right time, making sure the music was playing at the right time and taking care of a multitude of responsibilities. During the second half, I left my post during media timeouts to go up into the stands and look for kids that I thought might be students. When I found them, I thanked them for coming and told them; *Hey, you know what? If we win this game, you're going to storm the floor.* They looked at me as if I was crazy. Bewildered, they asked, *We can do that?* I said, *Absolutely you're going to do it!* I told them, *Under 4 minutes, if we are winning this game and there's a timeout called, I want you to go meet up underneath that basket down there.* While the game was going on I kept scanning the crowd for students, and I went out into the stands during the 16-minute timeout, the 12-minute timeout, and the 8-minute timeout.

I also had the department camera and was taking crowd shots so we could update our gym images. We hit a big three late in the game and I got an amazing picture of the crowd standing up, cheering. We got down to the final minutes of the game and there were close to 20 students gathered under the basket. When the final buzzer sounded, the score was 37-35 (high-scoring affair) in our favor and they rushed the floor as requested after getting the nod from me. It was like the running of the bulls in Pamplona. They were jumping up and down at mid-court with the team as if we had won a major championship. It was one of the coolest moments I have ever been a part of from a college athletic standpoint. Granted, we might have had as many players and staff on the floor as we had students, but that mid-court celebration was a poignant moment. It was a huge deal for our players, our students and the rest of the fans who came out. We got some great pictures too, although we had to crop them to make it look like a bigger mob scene than it actually was. That night, our win even got a mention on the *SportsCenter* crawl, as it was a major upset.

Even though it was a small game compared to some of the big moments I've been a part of such as the College Football playoff, Final Four and national championships, it was the first time I'd ever really had that euphoric feeling after a game. I could not sleep that night because I was still amped up from the game. I just kept reliving that moment in my head and picturing the smiles on our student-athletes' faces. To me, that night was all about living in the moment, being thankful for what you have, and connecting with fans. As I have gone on to work at larger programs, I have never forgotten what it is really all about.

NO PLACE LIKE NEBRASKA

• • • • • • •

CHRIS PLONSKY

Director of Women's Athletics and the Executive Senior Associate AD for Men and Women's External Services
University of Texas

It was 1998, and the University of Texas was in its third football season as a member of the Big 12. Mack Brown was in his first year as head coach, and we'd been fortunate enough to have Ricky Williams decide to stay with us for his last year of eligibility.

On a brutally cold Halloween day, we played #7 Nebraska at their stadium in Lincoln. Nebraska was on a 40-game winning streak for conference games; they had been seemingly unstoppable since 1992. The odds were stacked heavily against us, but our guys gave it everything they had and just played off the charts. Ricky didn't have one of his 300-yard days, but I think he got maybe a buck-fifty or a buck-fifty-seven. Every single yard was hard-earned on that cold turf against Nebraska's legendary Blackshirts defense. In the end, we pulled the game out dramatically to win 20-16.

After a little hoist in the air for Mack, the rest of our team jogged into the locker room to get warm and celebrate our victory while Mack and Ricky stayed on the field to do an interview with ABC. Between the freezing weather and the stunning loss for Nebraska, I would have expected the stands to empty out quickly, yet the Nebraska fans waited in the stands above the end of the tunnel to our locker room so they could applaud Ricky when his interview was done.

What a moment of incredible sportsmanship! Those fans had just had their hearts busted. They had cheered their team mightily, and they'd had no reason to expect anything but victory that day. It must have been agonizing for them to have their winning streak broken by an unranked opponent, but they knew they had witnessed a historic effort. I remember looking up and thinking, *Now, these are fans.* Their stomachs had to be hurting, yet they lined the railings and made sure our superstar and our coach knew how much they admired and respected the effort we'd put forth.

Ricky was a young guy who probably didn't look like many of the players on Nebraska's team. He had dreadlocks, he had his own style, and he just had a free spirit. But those fans didn't judge him and they didn't resent him for taking the win away from them. They waited there in the cold to show how much respect they had for how he went about his business of being a leader for our team.

I remember thinking, *If every fan of college athletics could take a lesson from Nebraska and what they just did!* It was the epitome of what sports is all about. I have always thought of that day as sort of a signature moment in Big 12 history where two great teams played, but Nebraska's fans stood up and were truly the class act.

Some games, it's just your day no matter how well the other team has been playing. For the fans to respect that, and to show that respect to our kids and coaches even while they're absorbing the disappointment of their own team's loss, teaches us so much about sportsmanship and says so much about their institution.

Some rivalries are bloody and disrespectful, and that's unfortunate. That takes away from the experience for everyone. Other times when teams play, you can just sense the mutual respect between them. The fans have a big role in that and you can really feel the difference. Unfortunately it's atypical, but that difference matters. It matters not only because of how great the competition is going to be, but also because it's an opportunity for the pride of the fans and the alumni to shine. It says a lot about an organization. When that type of game happens, it's good for the athletes, it's good for the fans and it's good for the institutions themselves. It's good for college sports as a whole. It's a different message, and when it happens you can just feel the buzz.

FORWARD TOGETHER

• • • • • • •

DANNY WHITE
Vice President and Director of Athletics
University of Central Florida

When I was the head of the Athletics Foundation at Ole Miss, we had a pretty big wish list: build a new basketball arena, make significant enhancements to the football stadium, create the kind of facilities that other SEC schools have. People had said for years that these things couldn't be done at Ole Miss. The presumption was that large capital projects were unreachable there because it's located in the poorest state in the country and they didn't have enough wealth in their fan or alumni base to raise the money we needed.

Despite all the doubts, we didn't let the naysayers stop us from trying. We launched a fundraising initiative called the "Forward Together Campaign" with the goal of raising $150 million dollars. Instead of putting a timeline on it, we basically just said, *Here's everything we're going to need to be really competitive in the SEC and we're going to let funding determine how quickly we knock out these projects.* That was a bold move for our department, and Chancellor Dan Jones and Athletic Director Pete Boone showed a lot of courage in letting us take that approach. We initially expected a little bit of a negative reaction from the alumni base because we had set such aggressive philanthropic goals, but the response we got couldn't have been better. It was overwhelmingly positive!

It was amazing to see a really high volume of dollars committed to that campaign in a very short period of time. I think one of the things that made it so unique was that we didn't have a single eight-figure gift. There weren't even very many substantive seven-figure gifts. Instead, there was just an incredibly high volume of smaller gifts from alumni who were really strong supporters of the university. It was truly impressive to see how everyone came together and supported each other and the school. Everyone gave what they could. What we might have lacked in major donors we made up for with a hundred years of tradition and an extremely passionate alumni base.

Working with the donors at Ole Miss made an enormous impression on me personally and on my entire family. A lot of people stepped up, and we had the opportunity to hear their stories about why Ole Miss mattered so much to them. I think that's the type of thing that leads to an athletic department's success. It's not about an individual game or an individual season, it's about galvanizing support for a shared vision. Ole Miss was able to do that at an unprecedented level. I never imagined the campaign would be as successful as it was so quickly, and I think that experience just speaks to how meaningful the passion of fans can be. Fans truly are participants in the overall success of an athletic program.

THE CLEMSON FAMILY

• • • • • • •

DAN RADAKOVICH
Director of Athletics
Clemson University

Throughout my career I've had the opportunity to learn from some truly great colleagues and mentors. When I worked at the University of Miami, baseball coach Ron Fraser coined the phrase "The Happiest Team in America" as he led our team to the National Championship. He showed me how camaraderie can propel a good team to greatness. When I worked at Louisiana State University, Athletic Director Skip Bertman taught me about customer service and relationships with your fan base. He was one of the all-time great baseball coaches, but more importantly he was a terrific person who understood the importance of taking care of fans. Those experiences taught me a lot about the value of winning the right way, and how incredibly important it is both to a school and to a community.

Here at Clemson, one of the things on which we really pride ourselves is the culture we've created over time. We put a lot of emphasis on the "Clemson Family" and having a great game-day atmosphere. Over the past three years we've had Louisville, Notre Dame, and Pittsburgh come to Death Valley. Notre Dame hadn't been here since 1979 and it was the first time Louisville and Pittsburgh ever visited. The letters, texts and other correspondence we got after those fan bases had experienced Clemson reiterated that our fans really do treat visitors incredibly well. They have a good time and they're very knowledgeable about their sport, but they also go out of their way to make sure visitors have a great experience too. It's not that we're inviting them to tailgates or anything; it's more the effort we make to approach people with other colored shirts and say, *Hi, do you know where you're going? Can we help you get there?* Making them feel welcome in our environment is something we take a lot of pride in.

For me, that's one of the reasons why our win at the 2016 College Football Playoff was so powerful. The last time Clemson won a football national championship was 1981. For decades, our fans have stayed true to us and, through all the ups and downs, they've extended a gracious welcome to everyone we've ever played. When we beat Alabama 35-31 in Tampa for the National Championship this year, it was incredibly moving to look up into the stands at the 20,000 fans who came to cheer for us and see the sheer joy on their faces. It was just so gratifying to see all these people who invested so many years in supporting our program experience such happiness. A member of our Board of Trustees who played on the 1981 National Championship team has a son who's currently a member of the Clemson football team, and seeing them share that moment and experience the same thing across generations was the epitome of what it means to be part of the Clemson Family. It was extremely poignant and really powerful.

When you're an athletic administrator you get a lot of internal satisfaction from seeing student-athletes grow and mature into great young men and women during the four years that they're at your institution. You see how much the institution means to so many people who invest their time, money and resources. All of those things together are what define a university and that's what drives us. It's the gratification that really keeps you waking up in the morning and coming to work to try to make it all better.

THE EXORCIST & A BLACKOUT

• • • • • • •

BRAD WURTHMAN

Senior Associate Athletics Director,
External Operations
Virginia Tech

I started my collegiate athletics career at the University of Cincinnati, and there are two moments that stand out most in my memory. They're both moments when fans rallied around the team, and I believe those fans made a difference in the outcome of the game.

In 2008, we played a Thursday night ESPN football game against South Florida. We had a talented team but South Florida was ranked 23rd and had been playing really well. They were definitely the biggest program in the league at that moment, while our Bearcats were fighting tooth and nail to stay relevant. The game was the night before Halloween and we sold out Nippert Stadium, an anomaly for Cincinnati in those days. All the in-town stars were there. We had players from both the Cincinnati Reds and Cincinnati Bengals show up; Erin Andrews was there with the ESPN crew. You had sky cam and all these other things that Cincinnati had never had at a game before so it became a really big deal for us.

At the time, we were a school that didn't have a lot of football traditions. That night, we inadvertently created one. Because it was so close to Halloween, we played the theme song from the "Exorcist" before kickoff and the theme song from the Michael Myers movie "Halloween" on third downs. The crowd loved it! The stadium was packed and it was as if our fans were willing a victory to happen. Our players on the field could feel it and they played their hearts out. After we won that game 24-10, "Halloween" became our tradition. To this day, that's still the song that's used on third downs. It doesn't have to be the day before Halloween; it can be the middle of September, the end of November or a random Saturday in early October. No matter who the Bearcats are playing or when, that's the song that's still used because it resonates with people.

I also remember a basketball game when we played Louisville as part of a Big East Conference home-and-home series. Louisville is one of Cincinnati's top rivals in any sport, but their rivalry in basketball is historic. At this particular game, both teams were ranked. We were playing at home, so we encouraged all of our fans to wear black and create a blackout. That night, the gym was the loudest it had ever been. The air was just charged with the intensity and enthusiasm of the fans. They were cheering so hard that it seemed like the place would explode! In the middle of the game, the public address announcer leaned over to me and said, *I think I see things falling from the ceiling.* The place was legitimately rocking, and the gym was old enough that we were worried the fans might actually bring it down! It was one of those moments where everything just came together. The game was over for Louisville before it even began that day, which you can't say very often about that team, as the Bearcats went on to upset Louisville 60-56.

In both cases, it was great to see what a fan base can do when they rally around a cause. Those two nights, the teams we were playing just weren't going to win no matter what they did. The combined power of our fans and our team was too strong. It makes you realize how much what we do means to the fans and also how much the fans themselves help bring it all together for the team.

CURVEBALLS

• • • • • • •

DAVE HART
Vice Chancellor and Director of Athletics
University of Tennessee

In 1991 we had the best football season in East Carolina University history. It didn't start off so great because we lost our opening game to Illinois. We were behind in the fourth quarter, then we recovered an on-side kick near their sideline and cut their lead to a single touchdown. It was an unbelievable comeback and our players were jumping up and down on the sideline in excitement. That's actually what did us in, because 1991 was the first year the celebration penalty rule went into effect. We received a penalty that put us at first and 25 instead of first and ten and it cost us the game. We learned from it though, and that ended up being our only loss of the season.

We won our next eleven games, including multiple victories over ranked teams. A lot of those wins were miraculous last-minute upsets, but we pulled it off every time. There sure were a lot of anxious moments for our fans. They've always been a passionate group and that season they started using, *We believe!* as the ECU catch-phrase. They would chant it at games and we had a local vendor who made purple, white and gold stick-ons that said it. Those wins might not have come easy but they couldn't have been any more exciting.

Our record got us into the Peach Bowl in Atlanta, which was a pretty big deal for East Carolina at the time. What made it even better is that we got to play NC State, our archrival from just down the road in Raleigh. With eight minutes left in the game, we had fallen significantly behind NC State. They had a 34-17 lead on us and it didn't seem like there was enough time left for us to recover. Things looked so hopeless that a lot of people left the stadium and were on the way back to North Carolina, listening to the finish on the radio instead of waiting for our seemingly inevitable defeat.

All of a sudden, they shanked a punt and this unbelievable finish began to unfold. The crowd started to chant, *We believe! We believe!* Even my mother-in-law was chanting it up in the box where we were watching the game. As *We believe!* filled the air, our team started making an impossible comeback. It was eerie, almost like you could see the passion of our fans actually helping turn the tide of the game. I'll never forget that feeling; experiencing it gave me goosebumps. In the last few seconds we won the game 37-34.

I think the thing that made that win and really our entire season so special was the belief our fans had in us. They weren't going to give up on the team and their support gave our players extra energy to make those amazing comebacks. I always tell student-athletes that life doesn't throw all fastballs: life throws curves; it throws sliders; it throws brush-back pitches, too. Sometimes you have to get out of the way, but then you get back in the batter's box and give it everything you've got. You don't run and hide when things aren't going your way. Knowing your fans have that type of perseverance too creates an amazing dynamic. I feel fortunate to have worked at places that have that level of passion.

FOURTH QUARTER
THE PLATFORM

In 1948, a white-only political group known as the National Party regained power in South Africa and began a 46-year reign as the ruling party, instituting policies of racial segregation and discrimination known as apartheid. Public facilities and social events were segregated and housing and employment opportunities were decided based on race. This was intended to maintain political and economic control of South Africa by the white minority. Entire tribes of black South Africans were relocated to "homelands," which were designated as independent nations, in order to create a white majority in the country. Black people were kicked out of government, stripped of their citizenship and forbidden to purchase or lease land in more than 90% of the country. Black males weren't even allowed in certain parts of the country unless they were employed there.

The African National Congress (ANC) is South Africa's social democratic party and has long stood in opposition to the policies of the National Party. The president of the ANC during this time was a lawyer from the Xhosa ethnic group named Madiba. After the National Party established apartheid, he and the ANC committed themselves to its overthrow. He spent the next decade working to end apartheid and was repeatedly arrested for seditious activities. Finally, in 1962 he was arrested for conspiring to overthrow the state and sentenced to life imprisonment. In South Africa he is still most often referred to by his Xhosa name. To the rest of the world, he is known as Nelson Mandela.

Mandela served 27 years in prison until international pressure and fear of a civil war prompted the government to release him in 1990. Upon release, he helped negotiate an end to apartheid and in 1994 became president of South Africa. He spent the rest of his life working for human rights causes including land reform, combating poverty and expanding healthcare services. He declined a second presidential term but went on to create the Nelson Mandela Foundation to promote HIV/AIDS prevention.

By all accounts, Nelson Mandela was a great man who spent his life fighting for noble causes. He was effective in his fight because public outrage over his 27-year imprisonment gave him an international platform to effect change. I still remember when he was released from prison and being in awe of what he'd done and been through. He could have spent his remaining years making up for lost time by relaxing and enjoying life. Instead, he used the platform he'd been given to make the world a better place.

In addition to being an unbelievable humanitarian, Mandela was also quite a sports fan. He said, *Sport has the power to change the world. It has the power to inspire. It has the power to unite people in a way that little else does.*

Nelson Mandela recognized in sports what we recognize in him. Sports has the platform to effect change. Sports isn't an American thing. Sports is an everywhere thing. And it is the responsibility of every one of us to utilize that platform to make the world a better place.

⑪

CHAPTER ELEVEN
WHEN PRESSURE IS APPLIED

❝ **Character is revealed when pressure is applied.** ❞
- Anonymous

In some parts of the world where there has been volcanic activity, you might find an igneous rock formation called kimberlite. Kimberlite forms about 100 miles below the earth's surface (feel free to check for yourself). Much of the kimberlite that was formed millions of years ago has made its way closer to the surface of the earth but the majority of it still lies well below your finely manicured lawn. Inside the kimberlite, you might find chains of carbon atoms that over the course of 1 to 3 billion years, and through a lot of intense pressure, became crystallized. Some pieces of kimberlite contain these pockets of crystallized carbon atoms. Some don't. It's only through taking a piece, chiseling away the rough exterior through a painstaking process, pulling out these carbon atoms, and then polishing them and shaping them into something beautiful that you end up with diamonds. The hardest, most beautiful and most valuable gem on earth takes years to develop. You have to dig deep to find them and then chisel away all of the exterior through a long and difficult process to discover what's inside. And sometimes, you find that there's nothing in there at all.

Sports do not build character. They reveal it.

That quote is often attributed to John Wooden but it's believed to have originated with journalist Heywood Broun. It's also a favorite of former Nebraska Head Football Coach, Tom Osborne, as you'll see. Regardless of who said it first, it's accurate. Character is like a diamond and the process for revealing it is pretty similar. An individual's character can be the most beautiful thing within a person. It takes years to develop and sometimes you don't know what's in there until you dig deep and go through something really painstaking. You tear away the rough exterior to see what lies beneath. Sometimes you discover something amazing inside. Sometimes what you find in there isn't quite as great as you had hoped.

Sports puts its participants through everything life can throw at a person. Winning, losing, pushing the limits of one's physical and mental capacity, forcing one to play as a part of a team... the list goes on for miles. There's absolutely nothing else in life that puts all of those things together in one package. Because of that, there's nothing else in life that reveals character like sports.

Winning can reveal humility and grace. It can also reveal arrogance. Losing can reveal strength and dignity. It can also reveal entitlement. Being pushed to one's limits can reveal toughness and courage. It can also reveal resignation.

Sports can reveal a lot of things. But nothing more than one's character.

The stories in this chapter are tales of times when these men and women faced adversity and became better for it. Times when they observed the character of athletes and were influenced by it. And stories of when the character of certain individuals became visible to all because of the platform that sports provided.

BROOK BERRINGER

• • • • • • •

TOM OSBORNE
Former Head Football Coach and Director of Athletics
University of Nebraska

Too often, you hear people say that athletics builds character. It can. But I think probably more than anything athletics tends to reveal character.

In 1994, our number one quarterback at the University of Nebraska was a young man named Tommy Frazier. About three games into the season, Tommy developed some blood clots down the full length of the back of one of his legs. We were told he wouldn't play any more that year and that he might never play again. It was a difficult moment for Tommy and for our entire team.

With Tommy sidelined, we turned to our backup quarterback, a junior named Brook Berringer. Brook was from a small town in western Kansas and had probably never played in front of more than 300 or 400 people at a football game. That's a lot different than what he would face in our games. When we started him at our next game, we didn't really know what to expect. We just hoped he would play well like he had in practices. The first game that Brook played, he took a hit in the back that partially collapsed his lung. But Brook was determined to keep going. He played through the injury and finished the game, leading our team to victory over Wyoming. The next week we were up against Oklahoma State. Brook played again, and again he got hit hard in the back, deflating his lung a second time. The doctors said that if it happened a third time, he would be done for the year.

It was only about halfway through the season and we were down two quarterbacks. Our next game was against Kansas State and we had to start our third-team quarterback. It was a tough game. In the second half, Brook said he wanted to play. He knew it was a risk, but he wanted to be on the field. So we put him in and used him in ways that we hoped wouldn't get him hit. We ended up winning 17-6, and Brook went on to play the rest of the season. We won the rest of our games that season. He played so well and led the team so effectively that we won the 1994 National Championship against Miami in the Orange Bowl.

The next year, Tommy Frazier had recovered and was ready to start playing again. We had a difficult decision to make, because Frazier had been the starting quarterback when he got hurt but Berringer had taken us to the National Championship. They were both excellent players, but they couldn't both be the starting quarterback.

So we simply threw things open in the fall camp. We graded every snap they had in scrimmages, every pass they made in practice, and so on. They were both working hard for it. In the end, Frazier had just a slight edge. I think Brook had thrown one interception in a scrimmage and Tommy hadn't thrown any. Tommy became the starting quarterback again and Brook didn't start another game that year.

Both Tommy and Brook had supporters among the other players, guys who thought one or the other was the better quarterback. It could have split the team and caused a lot of tension, but Brook didn't allow that to happen. He put the team ahead of himself. Even though you could tell it hurt him not to have the starting position, he stood on the sideline and supported Tommy. He said the right things, did the right things, and held the team together. Brook kept a positive attitude and played the role he had to play. You could tell he was a person of strong faith, and he was certainly made of the right stuff. We won all of our games again that year, in part because we had such a great supporting cast.

About two or three months after the season was over, Brook was getting ready to graduate. Things were going really well for him: he was engaged to be married and he looked good for the NFL Draft. He probably would have been drafted in the middle round, fourth round, somewhere in there. Everyone's hopes were high.

Brook wanted to be a pilot, so he talked some local guy into letting him fly a little Piper Cub. It was a beautiful spring day, and Brook took his future brother-in-law out for a flight. While they were in the sky, the engine quit. Brook tried to turn back to the landing strip but the wind caught the plane. There was nothing Brook could do; the plane went down like a kite. It hit the ground and burned, and both Brook and his prospective brother-in-law died in the crash.

Having somebody like Brook taken away so suddenly at such a young age impacted a lot of our players. When you're 18, 19, 20 years old, you think you're going to live forever. I think a lot of our players always kind of assumed they were bulletproof. Losing Brook was a wake-up call. It made all of us think about what was important in life and what it took to make Brook the kind of person that he was.

We took three or four busloads of players down to Brook's funeral in Goodland, Kansas. As we were driving there, we saw people standing all along the highway with signs and flowers for Brook. They didn't know him personally, but they were there out of respect for the person he had been and admiration for how he had lived his life. His life - even though it was relatively brief - impacted not just our players but also an awful lot of Nebraskans. They all recognized the strength of his character and the type of person he was and what he stood for in life.

For me, that event encapsulated the influence and the power of athletics. Athletics can be a powerful influence for good, for what's right, and for the best in all of us. I think it's important to remember the original intent of athletics, which is simply testing yourself in a competitive environment and trying to grow and become all that you can be, not just athletically but also in terms of character and personality and influence. If someone is given the platform of athletics, it's incumbent upon them to use that position in a constructive way. Brook showed us what that looked like.

WHAT ELSE?

• • • • • • •

CHRIS PLONSKY
Director of Women's Athletics and the Executive Senior Associate AD for Men and Women's External Services
University of Texas

My family lived in Greensburg, Pennsylvania when I was young. I grew up with really bad allergies, so my dad would have to take me into Pittsburgh to get allergy shots. On our way home, he would always figure out a way to stop at old Forbes Field around the fourth inning of a Pittsburgh Pirates game so we could get in free and watch the last few innings. I loved going to those baseball games; they made going to Pittsburgh something to look forward to instead of something to dread. I even remember asking for a baseball glove when I was five. I grew up knowing who Roberto Clemente, Willie Stargell, Bill Mazeroski, Smoky Burgess and all those guys were.

When we moved to Ohio in the late '60s, I stayed a Pirates fan. Even though we didn't live near Pittsburgh any more, I did everything I could to keep up with the team. My dad and I used to lay on the living room floor and tune in KDKA Radio to listen to Bob Prince and Nellie King calling the Pirates games play-by-play. I adored Roberto Clemente because of his style and the way he played with such reckless abandon. He was fast and had a rocket arm, and it was incredible how he could lash out a hit. Even though he was a minority in the 60s (from Puerto Rico), the clubhouse and the community embraced his quiet, solid leadership. He was revered both in his homeland and by the fans in Pittsburgh for leading the team to multiple championships.

On New Year's Day 1973, I woke up to the news that Roberto Clemente had perished in a plane crash while taking goods to the victims of a Nicaraguan natural disaster. I was in complete shock. I was about 14 at the time and had no experience with death, and to me, somebody like Roberto Clemente had seemed untouchable. It was hard to believe that this hero, this person I admired not only for his athletic prowess but also for the way he handled himself and the way he represented his sport, was gone forever. That's not how life was supposed to be!

Listening to the news coverage and reading the stories that followed his death, I saw that people missed him far less for his athletic exploits than for the compassionate human being and strong leader he had been. What made him irreplaceable wasn't his skill at baseball, it was the fact that he was a person who had done so much for others. I started to understand that sports wasn't just about winning and achievements, but also about the greater good you could do through the visibility athletics gave you. His death made me realize that's the way that sports was supposed to be, that somebody participating in sports should leave that kind of legacy.

When we recruit student-athletes, hire coaches or work with staff, we always are looking for that intrinsic *what else* within. What do they deliver as a person, as a human being? You look for values, morals and leadership; the ability to be humble and yet be a leader; to play a key role but to be willing to self-sacrifice for the greater good. That's what Roberto Clemente sort of shouted in his quiet and humble way. That's what really matters.

DIG DEEP

• • • • • • •

KIRBY HOCUTT
Director of Athletics
Texas Tech University

Growing up in the state of Texas, all I wanted to do was play big-time college football. It's something I had dreamed about for as long as I can remember. Receiving a scholarship offer to attend Kansas State University allowed me to realize that dream, and the five years I spent as a part of that program were really impactful. I was surrounded by great educators, coaches, mentors, leaders and teammates. That experience still influences what I do each and every day today as an athletics director, as a husband, as a father and as a professional.

When I got to Kansas State, we weren't the strongest team around. The first three years I was there were building years for the program. We didn't have a great record during that time, but we were getting better and we started to succeed more and more. I was very fortunate to be a part of what I consider one of the greatest turnarounds in college football history.

During my junior year, I was starting at middle linebacker. Being on the starting lineup for a college team was everything I had aspired to do throughout years of watching and playing football as a kid. It felt pretty amazing to actually reach that goal. Partway through that season, though, we had a game against a really good Colorado team and I just didn't play very well. It wasn't my best game by a long shot. The Sunday after that game, I walked into the film room and Coach Leavitt looked at me and said, *Kirby you're not starting next week. I'm starting DeShawn Fogle.*

I couldn't believe what I was hearing. I'd worked for that starting position my entire life! It meant everything to me, and having it taken away was a shock. I forget who we played the next week, but I realized that I had a decision to make. I could pout or I could go back on that practice field on Monday and get my starting position back. I remember our Co-Defensive Coordinator Bob Stoops putting his arm around me and saying, *Hey, you've got to keep your chin up. Come out and do what you've been doing all year and you're going to be just fine.*

By midway through the first quarter of the following game, I was back on the field. Nothing was going to stop me. That year, I led the Big-8 in tackles and was fortunate enough to receive All Big-8, All-Conference honors. I never lost that starting position again.

That was the year all of our hard work finally paid off, and it was the most successful season our program had experienced in 83 years. We ended up ranked in the Top 20 and got to go to the Copper Bowl in Tucson, Arizona. It was the first time in 25-plus years that Kansas State had made it to a bowl game and only the second bowl game ever in K-State history. As we ran out onto that field in Tucson, Arizona, one entire side of the stadium was solid purple. It was incredible! Looking up at that sea of purple, I remember thinking, *Wow, what an awesome turnout and support that we have.* We beat Wyoming 52-17, winning Kansas State's first-ever bowl game victory. I had this feeling of awe at being part of such a historic moment in the resurrection of Kansas State Football.

That game was one of the most memorable experiences of my life, and I would have missed out on it if I hadn't made the decision to put the work in and earn my position back. It taught me that when you're faced with adversity, you have to make the decision to dig deep rather than just give up. The long practices, the challenging days, the times that you didn't feel like you could go any further or that you could be pushed any more… that's when you had to look to your teammates and just persevere. Those are the moments that form bonds, relationships, and memories that nobody can take away from you. They end up being your most valuable experiences.

As a student-athlete, you not only get a world-class education but you also get to learn leadership lessons and grow as a person while competing in the sport you love. You learn that consistency and commitment to the process - doing the best you can do, each and every day - will lead to favorable results. The adversities that you face later in life are no different. There will always be challenges. You've just got to remain consistent to your purpose and your guiding principles, surround yourself with good teammates, and commit yourself to achieving your goal.

SMALL MOMENTS

• • • • • • •

ALLEN GREENE
Director of Athletics
University at Buffalo

I can think of so many small moments throughout my life where athletics played a part in shaping me to be who I am today. When I was around five years old, I was on a T-ball team. We had to play multiple positions so I might have played third base one inning, right field the next and catcher after that. I wanted to win so badly, that I fielded balls all over the diamond. I eventually learned that I couldn't chase the ball every single time and that I had to rely on my teammates to do their part. The discipline and sense of teamwork I learned while playing T-ball is something that has stayed with me since that time.

I also played soccer growing up and I remember playing when it was cold, rainy and just miserable conditions. Through the entire game, our team complained about the weather. Finally, our coach basically said, *The other team has to play in this too. The less you worry about it, the better you're going to be and the greater advantage you're going to have.* Ever since then, I've thought no matter what the circumstance, my "opponent" has to deal with very similar challenges. It's up to me to block out the distractions and handle the situation better than the other person. By doing so, I give myself a competitive advantage.

I played high school basketball at O'Dea, an all-boys Catholic high school in the heart of downtown Seattle. My junior year we had a really great season and made it all the way to the State Championship game. I can't even remember who we played, but I remember it being a close game. In the final seconds, one of my teammates and a very close, lifelong friend missed a layup that would have either tied or won the game for us (my memory of the details is murky). I remember walking off the court and thinking, *Wow, if we'd only done a couple of things differently we could have won that game.* But as I looked over at my friend I could see how devastated he was, so I put my arm around him and said, *It's not your fault. It's fine, we'll be alright.* When the coach talked to us in the locker room, I kind of set my own emotions aside and focused on helping the rest of the guys on our team deal with the loss. Sport has taught me to, at times, suppress my own feelings for the sake of helping others.

As a sophomore in college, our baseball team was playing in the Big East Tournament in Norwich, Connecticut. I was 0-for-3 with three strikeouts and I left several runners on base. I was letting my team down. It was the bottom of the ninth when I stepped back up to the plate and I was struggling. I got down 0-2 with a runner on third base. If he made it in we would tie the game. Somehow, I managed to hit a single down the third base line scoring the tying run. During that final at-bat, I had to muster up every ounce of confidence I had to step into the box with positive thoughts. That experience taught me that even when the odds are against you, and you've failed several times over, you have to believe in yourself and keep trying.

Lastly, about four years ago we made the decision to fire our Men's Basketball Coach at the University at Buffalo. He was a long-time local legend and our athletic department took some heat for it; people said, *You shouldn't have done that. Show the guy more respect.* It was tough but we had to make a change because our program wasn't able to get over the hump. Two years later, we won the university's first Conference Championship and took our first trip to the NCAA Tournament. I remember being on the court afterwards and celebrating with tears streaming down my face. My colleagues, who had been at the university for ten-plus years and had never experienced this type of feeling before, were crying too. We all embraced and were all like, *This made it all worth it!* Winning that championship made up for all the naysayers and all of the people that didn't believe in what we were doing. It reinforced everything I've learned in life about not giving in to pressure, or taking the easy way out, rather making the decision you know is right for the betterment of your organization.

It doesn't matter whether you're playing on a local team as a kid or involved in athletics at a higher level, sports always has something valuable to teach you. I think that's one of the greatest things about it. Small moments in sports can have a lasting influence on someone's life; those moments give us each the opportunity to become better people.

WALKING THROUGH FIRE

• • • • • • •

WHIT BABCOCK
Athletic Director
Virginia Tech

Almost every single time you see a team win a championship, they mention having to overcome adversity to get to where they are. I think the challenges inherent in athletics teach people about character and persever-ance. The ability to get through the tough times is a contributor to team success. One of my most memorable experiences involves helping a team recover from a difficult situation.

My first Athletic Director job was at the University of Cincinnati and one of my first big games with the team was our rivalry basketball game against Xavier University. The two schools are only 3 miles apart, so the Crosstown Shootout is a really intense event; lots of emotion, and always a packed house. Xavier was hosting that year, so we played at their home, the Cintas Center.

At the game, I remember sitting in the front row behind our bench, right beside our President. Xavier was ranked No. 8 at the time, but our team didn't let that bother them. If anything, it just added fuel to their fire. You could practically feel the air vibrating from how intensely all the play-ers were wound. In the first half, there were six ties and eight lead changes with neither team letting the pressure off for a second. Just before halftime, things got a little heated between one of our players and one of theirs, so during the break the coaches talked to the kids about keeping their cool and staying focused on the game.

Xavier came back a lot stronger in the second half than we did. As the clock ticked down to 18.6 seconds, Xavier player Tu Holloway completed a layup to bring the score to 76-53. That's when all heck broke loose! Holloway made some comments to our bench and one of our players, Ge'Lawn Guyn, went over to confront him. The argument got physical and before anyone knew what was happening both benches had emptied and it had become an all-out brawl on the court! The kids were shoving and punching each other. It was complete chaos and I didn't know what to do. Again, the President was seated beside me the whole time. Nothing in my previous experiences prepared me for this! The coaches finally got in between the players and got their teams back under control, but it was so bad that the referees ended the game with 9.4 seconds remaining on the clock and Security had to escort the teams to the tunnels. When it was all said and done, two of our players were retroactively ejected from the game for fighting.

Coach Mick Cronin was furious and also embarrassed at how our players had behaved. The presidents of both schools issued public statements condemning the brawl, as did the Big East Conference and the Atlantic 10 Conference. The national scrutiny we were under was intense and everybody had something to say about what was going on. We ended up suspending four players for their behavior and Coach Cronin made sure everybody knew that even after the suspensions ended, those players would have to earn their way back onto the team.

That was an incredibly difficult time but we navigated it. We disciplined those players not just to punish them but also to try to teach them something. Those are the types of moments that shape people's lives, both on the team and off. Whether they realize it or not, our players influence others through the example they set. They weren't bad kids, they had just gotten caught up in the heat of the moment and acted out of character.

While those kids sat out their suspensions, the rest of the team rallied. They didn't want the team to be painted in a bad light and they poured a lot of energy into redeeming the Bearcats. We went on a winning streak and ended up going all the way to the Sweet Sixteen. I remember watching our players celebrate in the hallway after beating Syracuse in Madison Square Garden at the Big East Tournament. Knowing everything those guys had been through – from the incident to the discipline, the suspensions and the national scrutiny – made it really powerful to see them smiling and hugging each other in victory. Seeing that joy and celebrating with them is something I'll never forget; there was this sense that they had redeemed themselves. We had walked through the fire together and not only survived, but emerged better and stronger in the end.

MAURICE CLARETT

• • • • • • •

HEATHER LYKE
Director of Athletics
University of Pittsburgh

When I worked at The Ohio State University, we had a phenomenal young running back named Maurice Clarett. He had it all going for him: talent, charisma, work ethic and a million-dollar smile. As a freshman, Maurice scored 18 touchdowns, set a school record for yards rushed as a freshman, and helped the Buckeyes go undefeated to win the 2002 National Championship title. He was incredibly talented, and it looked like the sky was the limit for him. We all thought he had the potential to be a Heisman trophy winner, maybe even more than once.

But off the field, Maurice's story was not ideal. The reason he wore number 13 is just one example that illustrates what his life was really like. Maurice had gotten into trouble for the first time when he was a young child. He and a friend had broken into a house in Youngstown to steal something and were on the second floor when the owner came home. They panicked and jumped out a window, breaking the glass. Maurice got a big gash in his head and ended up getting 13 stitches. That's why he wore number 13. He had brushes with the juvenile court system throughout his youth yet when he came to Ohio State, Coach Tressel and I both tried to help him, to teach him right from wrong and hold him accountable. But Maurice struggled. At that time, he just wasn't mature enough to figure things out and he surrounded himself with some not-so-good people. Unfortunately, he ended up being suspended from the team in 2003 and later dismissed from the University.

When Maurice left Ohio State, he tried to pursue an NFL career but things didn't work out for him, so he went to the street and got involved in some extremely unfortunate situations. Maurice got in trouble for armed robbery in early 2006 and later that year he was pulled over and arrested after driving up the wrong side of a highway ramp in Columbus. He was literally on the wrong path, going the wrong direction, and ironically that's what ended up saving him from himself. When the police pulled him over he was wearing a bulletproof vest, had loaded guns in his car, and was on his way to even more serious trouble. Who knows what would have happened if they hadn't stopped him when they did?

Maurice was sentenced to 7 ½ years in prison. He ended up spending about 3 ½ years incarcerated and he used that time to turn his life around. He read everything he could, trying to better understand himself and why he had been making such poor choices. He spent time studying business, the economy, and anything else he could get his hands on. After being released early for good behavior, Maurice began sharing his story and became a much sought-after motivational speaker. In 2013, ESPN's 30 for 30 documentary "Youngstown Boys" featured his story. Maurice recently got approval to build a home in Youngstown for kids who get kicked out of juvenile court and don't have a place to go, a little bit like a halfway house. That's something he's really proud of.

I had lost contact with Maurice for a while, but when I was hired as the Vice President and Director of Athletics at Eastern Michigan his was the second text I received congratulating me. I didn't know he still had my phone number! It was great to hear from Maurice. About a year ago, I reached out to Maurice and said, *You know, my football team - they just don't get it. They're great kids and most of them make pretty good decisions so we don't have a lot of off-the-field situations, but their level of confidence is not where it needs to be. And I also don't think they believe in themselves as much as we believe in them. I know you're doing a lot of motivational speaking and public speaking but would you come up and talk to my team?* Maurice agreed and I got the chance to have a wonderful reunion with him and his long-term girlfriend, Ashley, who he had been dating since his time at Ohio State.

When Maurice spoke to our team, he was real with them and didn't hold anything back. A lot of our student-athletes were toddlers when Maurice was a star and then got in trouble so they didn't know his story, but he spoke in a way they could really identify with. Maurice explained his level of commitment to being the best and his confidence in his abilities never wavered. He told them, *There were times that young Maurice just reappeared and I made bad choices. Yeah, I won a national championship but look what I gave up. People like Miss Heather were trying to help me all along but I couldn't get past myself. I didn't listen to the right people who were trying to help me.* He talked to them about spending time in jail and he told them, *I don't know that I would be alive if I hadn't gotten pulled over when I did. I'm lucky to have a second chance.* The message resonated with the team. They connected with it and it changed them. We went from a 1-11 record to going to a bowl game the following year for the first time in 29 years.

You're not going to be able reach every kid when they're 18 to 22. You can't make their choices for them. But I believe you should never give up on them. If you're able to connect, powerful things can happen. Maurice Clarett may not have fulfilled his potential as a football player after that first national championship season at Ohio State, but the tragic side of his story is what allows him to connect with people the way he does. His involvement with sports has helped him overcome challenges and have an incredible impact today on other people's lives.

12
CHAPTER TWELVE
A MATTER OF OPPORTUNITY

> **Healing is a matter of time, but it is sometimes also a matter of opportunity.**
>
> *- Hippocrates*

I have two stepdaughters whom I love dearly. They are separated by a little more than 3 years in age but when they were little, they were inseparable. They played dress-up every day, they had tea parties and they adored each other. As time has gone by, of course, the older one has become a teenager and is more interested in teenage things. She has her social life, she has to study more and she has her obsession with volleyball. The school team, the club team, the all-day tournaments and the weeknight practices. Needless to say, the girls have grown apart a bit. But as luck would have it, the younger one decided to play volleyball this year through the city's recreational league. Big sister offered to help coach. Recently, at practice, the two were practicing serves next to one another. They were laughing and joking and carrying on, just like when they were little. Mom's heart swelled seeing them play together and laugh together like they had done every day when they were little. Their relationship hadn't been broken. It didn't need to be healed, per se. But there is a gap between them now that didn't exist when they were younger. Sports bridges that gap. Volleyball brought them back together, if even just for a few moments, in a way that nothing else has the power to do.

Hippocrates believed that while healing is a matter of time, it's also a matter of opportunity. I don't know if he was talking about physical healing, emotional healing or both. But I do think he hit the nail on the head with his quote. We've all heard the phrase, *time heals all wounds*. And that's true to an extent. Time may not completely heal all wounds but it certainly makes them more bearable. Opportunity, however, can significantly accelerate the healing time on wounds, and sports provides those opportunities in spades.

I went through a divorce in 2011. My sons were 8 and 4 at the time and it was the most difficult thing any of us had ever been through. I have always been a very involved father. From birth-through-kindergarten, I got my oldest son up every morning, got him ready and delivered to daycare because his mother had to leave for work before he was awake. I got up with them in the middle of the night for feedings, read to both of them every night before bed, was in charge of bath time most evenings, coached their teams and yes, took them to a lot of sporting events. I'm not bragging on myself. Just pointing out that I was accustomed to being with my boys a lot. So when all of a sudden I was put in a position where not only could I not put them to bed every night, I couldn't even see them for days at a time, it nearly killed me. I missed them, they missed me and a lot of tears were shed during this time.

I was living in a rickety old rent-house near Old Hat headquarters during this period and there was a big empty field right next door. On the days I had my boys, I'd take the afternoon off, get them from school and we'd spend the afternoon playing baseball in that field. The bases would be rocks or pieces of trash we'd found lying around. We'd have to play with "ghost runners" in order to get batters home. And somehow, I always seemed to lose.

The boys and I laughed as much or more than we ever had during those afternoon baseball games. There were home runs, high-fives, celebratory hugs after big plays... and at least one bloody-nose (sorry, Tace). All three of us were very much in need of healing that spring and our make-shift baseball diamond provided it. The great thing is that as broken as we were, if you ask any of us to think back to that time, we don't focus on how painful of a time it was. We focus on all the fun times we had in that big empty field playing baseball.

Sports not only provides an opportunity for healing physical wounds but emotional wounds as well. Sports brings families, friends, and strangers together in ways that nothing else can. It makes friends out of strangers and can make broken families feel whole again. The stories in this chapter are some of the most powerful stories in this book. I went into this thinking I was going to hear all of these stories about winning that amazing game, coming back from being the underdog, etc. I had no idea that I was going to be on the verge of tears while listening to someone tell their story of the times they witnessed the healing power of sports. I hope that this chapter allows you to see the true power of sports and the power sports has to help people of all ages hurt a little less when they are in the depths of physical or emotional pain.

STORIES I DON'T KNOW

• • • • • • •

RICK HART
Director of Athletics
SMU

Society generally views the young men and women in our college programs just as athletes, but they're humans too. They have family issues, they have girlfriend-boyfriend issues, they have good moments and bad moments. To see the maturation and growth over four years, to see the person they become and watch them reach goals they never would have thought possible - that's where it begins and ends.

There are so many special sports-related moments that the public just doesn't see. They're moments that involve student-athletes, coaches, staff, and student-athletes' families. There are joyous moments, like families crying happy tears because a student who's about to graduate will be the first in his/her family to do so. There are moments of adversity, when you watch your student-athletes struggle through injuries or tough times. There are turning points, moments that help these young men and women define who they are and who they want to become.

But if you go beyond that and really see the impact of sports, not just on athletes, but also on fans and communities, it's even more powerful. Here are a few stories that reflect that.

Although 9/11 happened more than 15 years ago, it's one of the moments that stands out to me like it was yesterday. I was in Norman, Oklahoma, on my way in to work. We had a meeting scheduled that morning, and then the unthinkable happened. On our campus and across the country, people in our roles had to make decisions about whether to play or not play, how soon to go back to playing, and how to handle things on campus. What happened across the country with sports in the aftermath of that day really demonstrated the role that sports plays in our society as a rallying point and a release. The way athletics helped heal and bring people together, restore a sense of normalcy, give people an escape… It was unbelievable.

Two years ago, SMU beat Tulsa in our last regular season game of the year and went on to our first Men's Basketball Tournament since 1993. To look around and see not just the jubilation of the team, but the pure joy and satisfaction of our alumni, our donors, and our community members, was amazing. That win meant so much to those 7,000 people in Moody Coliseum. To know what our program means to them, and the satisfaction and pride that they get from it, is very powerful. It made me happy we were able to give that feeling to the people who have invested time and energy and resources supporting our program and our student-athletes.

Recently, I got an email from a band member who I've known for several years. I didn't know a lot of his story beforehand, but he emailed me to let me know that his mom had lost her battle with cancer. He told me that she had been sick for several years, and that one of the things that kept her going - got her out of the house, lifted her spirits - was coming to our events. I'd had no idea we were making that kind of impact on their lives. For us, it was always just another game. For her, it was a lifeline of temporary reprieves on an incredibly difficult journey.

Thinking about my own personal experiences, I remember going to the Final Four numerous times with my dad. Those are memories that I've cherished for years. Now, having my own children attend events with me,

I know we are making memories as a family that will last a lifetime. And I've come to realize that we're not the only ones for whom sports offers that amazing opportunity. At every event, somebody is creating a memory that will stay with them forever.

When I look out in the stands, I sometimes just take a moment to appreciate all the stories I don't know about. I wonder what brought these people here and what role this event is playing in their lives, be it creating a lifetime memory or extending their family tradition or serving to heal or provide a moment of escape or inspiration.

Day to day, I'm inspired and driven and motivated by preparing our students for life. To know that we have an impact not just on the 424 young men and women in our athletic program, but also on entire communities, that's a very powerful thing. It's something I don't take for granted, so I try to pause to observe and appreciate it as often as I can.

FIFTY STARS & THIRTEEN STRIPES

• • • • • • •

KURT GULBRAND

Senior Associate Athletics Director for Development
University of Tennessee

In 2001, I was working for the University of Michigan and one of our first football games of the season was on September 8th at the University of Washington. I remember our fans being excited about it because fall is a great time to visit the Pacific Northwest. But on the Tuesday morning after our game, the tragedy of September 11th struck and everyone's lives changed in a significant and profound way.

We had been scheduled to play Western Michigan on September 15th, but the shock of 9/11 was still too fresh. The University of Michigan decided to postpone the game until our bye week, which was the following week. People everywhere were struggling to get back to the lives that they'd known, trying to regain a sense of normalcy after our world had been shaken to the core. There was this immense desire to experience what we do as a country, to cheer for a common purpose or experience a common thread and feel connected in a more positive way.

On September 22nd, with the pain of the attack still heavy in our hearts, the University of Michigan squared off against Western Michigan. When the color guard of service men and women brought the American flag onto the field, everyone in the stands stood up and began applauding. You could feel the pride and raw emotion swell throughout the stadium. As they hoisted the flag up and the marching band played the National

186 | If Not for Athletics - Fourth Quarter

Anthem, chills went through my body.

There were 109,000 fans there that day, and there wasn't a dry eye in the facility. It's the only time in my life where I've heard 109,000 people sing anything in unison, and every last one of them was singing at the top of their lungs. It didn't matter if you were off-key or off-tune. It didn't matter that those 109,000 people had different temperaments, beliefs, backgrounds, religions and politics. The only things that mattered were those 50 stars and 13 stripes, the service men and women on the field, and how much the words we were singing meant to the fabric of our country and our society.

That was a powerful and emotional time in our country. Everyone came together under our flag and our Constitution, and if you drove down any street in America, you saw American flags flying. You couldn't find an American flag in a store because they were all sold out. Regardless of their differences, people shared a belief in one thing: how great this country is, because in our country you're free. You have the ability to chase any dream, whether it be athletics or academics or something else. There's nothing you can't do in this great country.

To experience that patriotism standing in the stadium with friends and family, to share that deep sense of pride and conviction with others you didn't even know... it was so powerful. Everyone believed in this country and you could feel it. It was absolutely amazing, and thinking about it still gives me goosebumps today.

HEALING
TOGETHER

• • • • • • •

KATHY BEAUREGARD
Director of Athletics
Western Michigan University

In 2001, I served on the NCAA Committee for Football Bowl Certification. There were 15 of us on the committee and on September 11th we had all the representatives for different bowls meeting with us in the tallest building in Philadelphia. We were so focused on what we were doing that we had no idea terrorists had flown two planes into the Twin Towers just an hour north of us. Finally, some people knocked at the door and asked us, *Do you guys have any idea what's going on in the world?* We were clueless. When we turned on the TV we saw helicopters and burning buildings and information about the attacks on New York City and the Pentagon. A hijacked plane had crashed in a field only 30 miles south of us. Philadelphia was being evacuated so they could use it as an emergency center. We were stunned.

The night before, I had read a book to my son about where Philadelphia is and where New York City is. As I heard the news about the events unfolding around us, my thoughts immediately turned to him. *Was he okay and was he wondering whether I was okay?* He knew how close I was to everything that was happening. I wanted to get home to my son as fast as possible but there was no transportation; the city had been shut down and all the flights had been grounded. It was nearly impossible to get out of Philadelphia and I'd never felt more challenged in my life.

Beyond my immediate transportation issue, we were scheduled to play football against the University of Michigan in Ann Arbor the following weekend. I remember wondering, *How are we going to make that game happen under these circumstances?* Then my next thought was, *What is the most important thing in our lives right now?* It certainly wasn't a football game. We canceled all of our events on campus immediately. I remember watching church services on TV and being on the phone with Bill Martin, the Athletic Director at U of M. We agreed to postpone our game, then Troy changed a game and Ball State changed a game and it started this ripple of changes. Normally, it would be impossible for something like that to happen because scheduling games is a huge process, but the entire collegiate athletic community came together and found ways to make it work in response to the crisis.

When we played U of M at noon on Saturday two weeks later, it was the first athletic event in the country since 9/11. We were playing 30 miles from the Detroit airport at University of Michigan Stadium, the largest stadium in the country. As we got ready to start the game I remember seeing airplanes in the sky, flying in and out of the Detroit airport. Even though there was a no-fly zone over the stadium I just kept thinking, *Oh God please, don't...* It was terrifying. Between our fans and their fans there were more than 100,000 people there, so if somebody was going to target the first large gathering in America we were it. The courage and patriotism I witnessed that day was unbelievable. Nobody questioned whether we should play that game or be that team. They were all just focused on what we needed to do and determined to get it done.

When the two bands came out and played the National Anthem it was the most unbelievable feeling I've ever had. There was so much raw emotion in that stadium. I can't even describe it. People were bawling and holding onto each other for support. Even after the Anthem ended and the game began, the event just had this indescribable aura. I can't tell you the score of the game because that wasn't important. What mattered was seeing the teams lined up, hearing the band play, and giving all those fans in patriotic outfits the opportunity to hug each other, cry together, and start finding themselves again. We were a country that had been terrorized and that game gave everyone an opportunity to start getting back to their every day lives. It literally helped bring the world back to some kind of sanity.

For me, that game was an incredible example of how important sports is and the bond it offers people. It's not about coming out of each game with a win or reaching a certain score, it's about helping people relate to something bigger than themselves, share the deepest of emotions and find healing together.

OVERCOMING

• • • • • • •

DR. ADAM WALKER
Senior Associate Athletic Director
University of Memphis

My mom battled breast cancer while I was growing up, and sports was something that bonded our family together when we really needed it. Between me and my two older brothers playing sports, my family was always going to football games, track meets and basketball games. Our shared love of athletics helped all of us cope when times were tough.

We thought my mom had beaten the disease at one point but her cancer came back when I was in high school. Both of my older brothers had already graduated and moved out by then, so it was just me, my mom and my dad at home. Watching my mom go through that struggle was incredibly difficult. Because of everything my family was going through, I wasn't really thinking about my next step in life or where I was going for college. I was just focused on our family and school, and athletics served as a much-needed distraction.

During my junior year, a K-State track athlete named Mark Padfield came out and volunteer coached at my high school. I'd always idolized athletes growing up and thought, *Man, there's no way I could be like them.* But Mark encouraged me and told me I could do it. The idea of being able to play sports at the next level gave me something to hope for during a really difficult time in my life.

My mom passed away during my senior year. Because of her death,

I felt compelled to stay close to home so my dad wouldn't be alone but I also wanted to be a college athlete. I had missed most of the traditional recruiting process, so I reached out to Steve Fritz at Kansas State. He told me, *You know all the scholarships have been signed but I'd like to have you as a preferred walk-on.* So I stayed at home and walked-on the track team at Kansas State.

The first year I was at K-State I red-shirted, trying to get stronger, bigger and faster. A lot of work goes into being an athlete, especially when you're a walk-on. It's an hour-and-a-half every morning at 6 a.m. weights, class all day, then 2½ hour practices, team meetings, etc. They don't give you much besides sweats and shoes, because a lot of walk-ons don't make the team. It's definitely something you have to be passionate about.

As a red-shirt freshman I was able to travel with the varsity team. I really wanted to get a scholarship, and I asked Steve what it would take to get one. He said, *You need to score at our Big 12 Conference meet.* So I worked hard and that first year I was able to place 5th at Texas A&M and get on a partial scholarship. Each year I progressed, despite some setbacks with injuries, and ended up on enough scholarship to cover tuition.

My senior year, the Big 12 Indoor Track & Field Championship was held in Lincoln, Nebraska. That's when Nebraska was still part of the Big 12. I remember being very focused in the weeks leading up to it, and I was feeling great going into the competition. Knowing it would be my last Indoor Big 12 really made me appreciate what an opportunity I had. My dad was there – he would go to nearly every meet. He was excited to watch my last Big 12s.

At that meet, everything felt like it was in slow motion as I was warming up. In the moment when I was throwing, everything just seemed to connect and feel right. I ended up throwing over 20 meters, which is just over 65 feet, and qualified for USA Nationals. That was really big for me, a personal record, and it felt like everything came together right then to allow me to be able to finish that high. I was actually leading going into the finals and I remember thinking, *Oh, my gosh, I've got a great chance to win Big 12s!*

Unfortunately, I missed the Big 12 Championship title by 4 inches. My teammate Tarl Vetter beat me out. He had a better throw than me on his last attempt. We ended up going 1-2, and I was happy it was him and not somebody from another school who beat me. Standing up on that platform and getting the medal was an amazing experience. Even though I didn't have the storybook ending of going from walk-on to Big 12 Champ, it was incredible to finish my career in such a great way, qualifying for Nationals and later being named an Academic All-American. Afterward, I remember embracing my father and hearing him say something like, *I wish Mom could have been here but I know she's proud of you.* It was really a special moment for us, with a lot of tears of joy and tears of reflection, too. It's one of those memories I'll never forget.

For me, being a student-athlete was really about the experiences and gaining life-long friends. Working together as a team teaches you a lot about character and work ethic and overcoming obstacles, and as student-athletes we formed strong bonds and connections. Even though K-State is a fairly large university, it's also like a family. After I lost my mom, that family helped me heal when I needed it the most.

HANDS ON HEARTS

• • • • • •

JEFF BAIN
Athletic Director
Martin Methodist College

When my daughter Rachel was in elementary school, her best friend was a girl named Deanna Glossup. The week before they were supposed to start middle school, Deanna was diagnosed with an incurable form of cancer. It would have been her sixth grade year, but she never really went to middle school because she spent the next three years getting special treatments at Vanderbilt and fighting for her life. When she wasn't in treatment, her outlet was to come to sporting events at Martin Methodist College with Rachel or with her family. Deanna came to nearly every home game we had. When she got really sick, we let her family drive the car up onto the soccer field to make it easier for her to get out and watch.

All of our student-athletes either knew Deanna or knew about her. I think Deanna's situation struck a chord with all of them because they weren't that many years older than she was; she could have been their little sister. The day Deanna died, some of our seniors came to me and said, *What can we do for Deanna Glossup's funeral? Can we go?* There were over 300 student-athletes at the time and there was no way that many of them would fit in the church where her funeral was going to be held. I said, *The cemetery is probably less than a mile away from the church. What if we line the street with all our student-athletes when the cars drive away from the church and make the turn through town to go toward the cemetery?* They thought it was a great idea.

Our student-athletes didn't just go themselves, they also invited every-one else in the student body to join them. The day of Deanna's funeral we had 500 students lining the streets as the cars and casket traveled from the church to the cemetery. When they saw all of our student-athletes lining the streets with their hands on their hearts, the people in the cars broke down crying. It was an unbelievable show of support to a little girl who had committed so much to supporting our student-athletes over three years. That simple gesture of lining the street with their hands over their hearts was a unique and moving way to send Deanna off and show their support for her and her family.

That moment is something Deanna's family will never forget. Neither will I and neither will our student-athletes. I think it's an amazing example of how sports can mean so much more than just a win or loss on a score-board.

THE STADIUM MOVED THAT DAY

• • • • • • •

KURT GULBRAND
Senior Associate Athletics Director for Development
University of Tennessee

On Christmas Eve, a young man named Elliott Mealer was heading to mass with his girlfriend Hollis, his brother Brock, and his father. The three of them were planning to sing in the choir. But just outside Wauseon, Ohio, they were in a tragic accident. Elliott's father and girlfriend were killed in the wreck, and his brother Brock was paralyzed. Doctors told Brock he only had a 1% chance of ever walking again.

Elliott had signed with the University of Michigan just before the holidays, but after that horrific event he wasn't sure whether he would emotionally be able to handle going to college and being away from his family. So Rich Rodriguez, who was in charge of recruiting for the University of Michigan at the time, altered the scholarship to try to help the Mealers. He also talked with Mike Barwis, a wonderful strength and conditioning coach we had recently brought on staff at Michigan. Mike is a dynamic individual who believes in finding a way to yes. Through Elliott, they got to talking with Brock and realized he had a tremendous determination to walk again. Mike offered up the facilities at the University of Michigan to help Brock achieve this goal, and the Mealer brothers agreed.

There had to be at least 50 locations closer to home where Brock could rehab, but he would drive up from Ohio every day to work out at the University of Michigan Athletic Department with Mike and his staff. Brock would park his car, wheel his wheelchair up to Schembechler Hall, and try to use crutches to walk in to do his exercises. Mike had told him, *You're not allowed to bring your wheelchair into Schembechler Hall if you want to walk again. I need you to be mentally tough enough to be able to do that.*

At the time, the University of Michigan was going through a stadium renovation project to rebuild The Big House to add some luxury seating, expand accessible seating for our handicapped patrons, and create a better experience for everyone who attends University of Michigan football games. The rededication of the stadium was scheduled to take place at the September 4th, 2010 game against the University of Connecticut. About a year prior to that event, Rich made a deal with Brock that if he could walk, he would lead our team onto the field.

You'd see the sweat pour down the young man's forehead just trying to take a step. But Brock kept on working at it and pretty soon he was getting a little bit better each day. Think about the determination it took to continue moving forward even when doctors who are experts in their field said, *You have a 1 percent chance to ever walk again.* Watching Brock try to overcome those odds was incredibly inspiring. We all go through days where we feel like, *I can't run this extra mile or I can't do this extra push-up or sit-up or I can't accomplish this or I can't do that.* But Brock, along with Mike and his team, never gave in to *I can't.* They always found their way to *Let's try this,* or *I can,* or *Yes.* It inspired everyone in the Athletic Department. We would drive by Schembechler Hall and see Brock's wheelchair outside and know that he was in there, committed to doing something that they said he couldn't do.

On September 4th, 2010, wearing a blue shirt that said, *1%,* Brock led the team onto the field in front of a capacity crowd. His brother Elliott and their mother were there too. At the time, it was the largest crowd in Michigan history. There were 113,000 fans screaming in unison, cheering for Brock as he took each step toward that M Go Blue banner at mid-field, the M Go Blue banner that every student-athlete before him had run under. As Brock reached his hand up to touch the banner, there wasn't anyone in the stands without a tear running down their face. Everybody was cheering for a kid from Ohio to lead our team onto the field and accomplish something that the experts said couldn't be done. It was a phenomenal, moving experience. That day, the Michigan football team went on to a tremendous victory as well.

Those doctors might have been experts, but they didn't understand Brock's spirit and his will. Brock had incredible drive. I think everyone on Mike's team and in Brock's family learned and grew through each other's support and encouragement. Beyond that, Brock set an example for the rest of us. He helped us appreciate the things we take for granted and strive harder for the things that mattered to us. *Well heck, if Brock can overcome those odds, we can succeed at whatever everyday task we're trying to accomplish.* I truly believe that Brock helped other people accomplish things that they thought they couldn't do because of his spirit, his drive, and his initiative.

I've seen a lot of things happen where insurmountable odds were overcome through athletics. I've seen people come back and win games on last-second touchdowns and scores. Each time, the roar that would take place afterwards was deafening and inspiring, and it was awesome to experience. But at no time in my life have I ever heard a roar like the one I heard when Brock got to mid-field and reached up to touch the banner. I'll bet the stadium moved that day. You ask anybody that's been to a Michigan Football game and they'll tell you - that day was the loudest they've ever heard Michigan cheer.

⑬
CHAPTER THIRTEEN
EVERYONE YOU MEET IS JOE PARKER

"Everyone you meet is Joe Parker."
- Old Hat Guiding Principle #1

I was 23 years old and in my first week in my dream job as the graphic designer for the University of Oklahoma Athletics Department. My office was in Oklahoma Memorial Stadium, where Brian Bosworth had played and Barry Switzer had coached. I was on top of the world. Not only that, I got to spend every day getting paid to design stuff for what was, in my mind, the greatest athletic program on earth. It was absolutely surreal.

I still remember my first design project. Joe Parker was the Director of the Sooner Club at the time and he asked me to come to his office to discuss something he needed for the upcoming Big XII Basketball Tournament. It was a little black and white flier to be mailed out to all of the Sooner Club members telling them about the activities available for them outside the event in the Sooner Club tent. I remember exactly what it looked like and in hindsight, the design was embarrassingly bad. But Joe didn't complain about what I delivered to him. He was gracious and kind and appreciative.

Joe is a few years older than I am so between his age and his experience, I was quite intimidated by him. To me, he was somebody. And I was nobody. But Joe didn't treat me like nobody that day or any day since. Joe treated me with respect and I remember being floored by how nice he was.

Joe is now the Director of Athletics at Colorado State University. He was the first person I ever designed anything for at OU and he was the first person I called when I started Old Hat. He had left OU for the University of Michigan a few months prior so when I was looking to hang out my own shingle, I reached out to him to see if they had any work for me. Joe asked the athletics development staff at Michigan to give Old Hat a shot, which they did, and the University of Michigan became Old Hat's first client. Then Joe, in his disarming way, suggested that Mark Riordan, in a different area of the UM athletics department, give us a shot. He did, of course, and for more than a decade Michigan was Old Hat's top grossing client.

Mark Riordan went on to work at Texas A&M where he continued to use Old Hat and we developed KyleField.com which put us on the path to create numerous other capital campaign websites. Joe went on to Texas Tech University where he continued to influence his colleagues to use Old Hat and is now at Colorado State where we have been fortunate enough to continue to work with Joe and his staff. That single relationship, formed over the first athletics design project I ever did, has resulted in literally millions of dollars in revenue for Old Hat.

Years ago when we were creating our guiding principles, I wanted the first one on the list to be based on a philosophy that I'd been preaching for years. It's the idea that at any moment you might meet the person that can make or break your career. What if I'd screwed up that project for Joe when we first met? What if I'd been late or if I had done a bad job on it? Would I be sitting here today writing this book having had a successful career in athletics marketing? I told my staff that we should treat every project and every relationship as if that's the one that could change your life. *Everyone you meet is Joe Parker.*

On one of my first ever trips to Ann Arbor to visit with the people I'd been working with, I was sitting across from Joe in his office and we were talking about how things were going with my new business. Without warning, Joe picked up his phone and dialed someone. *This is Joe Parker calling for Chris.* I sat there and listened to Joe talk with someone on the other end. He told him about me and about Old Hat and how wonderful we are. He told Chris that his organization should give us a shot if they're ever in need. They talked for a few more brief moments and the call ended. *That was Chris Del Conte,* he said. Chris was the Director of Athletics at Rice University at the time. Rice eventually became a client of Old Hat's. We've also done work for TCU, where Chris is now, and he provided a great story for this book which you'll read in Chapter 14.

I remember being floored by that conversation and wondering how

Joe could just call up someone like that, encourage them to use a company they'd never heard of, and then have that person actually do it! But then I remembered who I was sitting across from. Joe had done so many nice things for me and always been so amazing to me that if he ever called me and said, *Zac! I know a guy that sells cars. He's the best. Next time you buy a car, you should buy it from him,* I would say, *Absolutely, Joe. Whatever you say!* And I'd do it, without question.

Joe Parker has the power of influence. To meet him is to love and respect him. And when you love and respect someone or something, it has the power to influence you. The more you love it, the more power it has to influence you.

What do thousands of people love more than almost anything? Sports. And because of our intense love of sports, it has the power to influence us more than almost anything else. When your favorite athlete wears Nike shoes, you wear Nike shoes. When Coach Larry tells you to eat at Larry's Barbecue, you eat at Larry's Barbecue. Teams, coaches and athletes have the power to influence us more than just about anyone else in our lives. If they didn't, the sponsorship industry wouldn't be the multi-billion-dollar industry it is today.

If sports can influence our purchasing habits, it can also influence us in very positive ways. That is what this chapter is about. So many times, athletes, coaches and teams are able to rally sports fans behind great causes and philanthropies. Whether it's a coach suggesting that we support the local children's hospital or a team donating their time to Habitat for Humanity, when we see these people we admire doing positive things, it influences us to do positive things. Fifty-three percent of respondents to our fan survey stated that at some point they were influenced to support a specific cause while attending a sporting event. That means that out of 80,000 people at a football game, 40,000+ of them might walk out of there willing to support something because their favorite team influenced them to do so! That doesn't even account for all of the people that were influenced in positive ways through advertising, press coverage, etc.

Joe Parker was the first person I called when I started this book project. I knew he'd agree to provide a story and I also knew that his participation would influence others to do the same. I started with Joe and more and more people agreed to be a part of it. The more people that agreed, the more others wanted to be a part of it. And just like when I started Old Hat, Joe helped me grow this into something huge.

People love sports and therefore, sports has an unbelievable power to influence. That power comes with responsibility. The stories in this chapter are about those times when athletic organizations used their power of influence for the greater good. Sports provides a platform for us to make a positive difference in the world. These are examples of times when it did just that.

LAUREN HILL

• • • • • • •

GREG CHRISTOPHER
Athletics Director
Xavier University

One night during the fall of 2014, I was watching the 11 o'clock news on one of the local Cincinnati TV stations. The broadcast included a story about Lauren Hill, a 19-year-old freshman at Mount Saint Joseph who had been diagnosed with DIPG, an inoperable and incurable form of brain cancer. Lauren was a basketball player and her biggest dream was to play in a college basketball game before she died. Mount Saint Joseph had requested and received permission from the NCAA to move the first game of their basketball season against Hiram College up a few weeks in order to allow Lauren to play.

Chris Mack, the Head Basketball Coach at Xavier, must have been watching the same channel because a few minutes after the story ended I received a text from him that said, *Hey, did you just see this story about this Lauren Hill? What do you think of playing that game at the Cintas Center?* I agreed and emailed Steve Radcliffe, the Athletic Director at Mount Saint Joseph, a note that said: *We're not trying to take this over in any way, this is your event and Lauren certainly is your player. I want to respect that. But if you need more space, please know that Xavier University would be glad to work with you to host this game.* The next morning Steve gave me a call. Lauren's story was quickly gaining national attention and as a small Division III school Mount Saint Joseph wasn't equipped to handle everything.

We agreed to move the game to Xavier's much larger arena and I volunteered our staff to help out.

The game was scheduled for November 2 and all 10,250 seats sold out in less than half an hour. The event was dubbed "Play for 22" to represent Lauren's jersey number and the two schools agreed to use the game as a fundraiser for The Cure Starts Now (TCSN) Foundation, a charity focused on DIPG research that was chosen by Lauren and her family. One of the things that was really fulfilling for me was seeing how our staff and student-athletes rallied around Lauren and Mount Saint Joseph. Watching each of our coaches and our 300 athletes get behind Lauren's cause in their own way, whether it was attending the game or helping raise money for the effort, was really uplifting. Even our ushers and the local police and fire departments donated their time so we could all maximize the money raised for charity at the game.

Tom Rinaldi was here for a week with his crew to do one of those signature three- or four-minute features that ESPN puts together. They put a lot of care into sharing Lauren's story in a transparent and honest way. It was unbelievably sobering and humbling to see how calm and positive Lauren and her family were throughout the weeks leading up to the game. I couldn't stop thinking about how hard it would be to be in her parents' shoes. It's one thing to walk out on the court and keep your composure while waving to a 10,000-person crowd, but it's another thing to maintain that strength behind the scenes during all the quiet moments and day-to-day challenges like the Hill family did.

The game itself was an incredible event. With the sold-out crowd of 10,250 it broke all attendance records for both Division II and Division III women's basketball. Lauren scored the first and last baskets of the game as Mount Saint Joseph defeated Hiram College 66-55 on national TV. During halftime, she received the Pat Summitt Most Courageous Award from Pat Summitt herself. Mount Saint Joseph ended up raising $40,000 for TCSN with that game, and since then we've continued to work with them and the Hill family to raise additional funding through an annual double header called the Lauren Hill Tipoff Classic.

Lauren passed away in April 2015. I can't say enough about Lauren's courage in facing the inevitable and her humility in using her situation as a platform for the greater good. Even though it was really sad, interacting with Lauren was uplifting to every single one of us. It made you think, *If this is how she faces something so terrible, how she literally faces death, how can we not go about our daily lives with more of a glass-half-full approach?* I may only have had the opportunity to know Lauren for three or four weeks, but her impact on all of us was amazing. Seeing the people I work with at Xavier come together to help Lauren, the Hill family and Mount Saint Joseph have an incredible experience that weekend, and to keep her legacy going through the tournament, is something that makes me truly proud.

SOMETHING GREATER

• • • • • • •

ANN ARGUST
Associate Athletic Director
University of Utah

No matter your age, your race, your religion or where you work, sport brings everyone together. I've seen it help people deal with national tragedy and I've seen it give people reasons for national celebration. To me, it's an honor to be a part of that.

Athletics allows us to help people in a lot of different ways. We're not just here to put on a game, we're a community partner. When we have the chance to make a difference for our community we absolutely need to do it. I think sometimes we don't realize how our programs can help other people outside of our own student-athletes. From giving people a way to come together in the wake of 9/11 to honoring our military to helping somebody overcome cancer, we have the opportunity to make some really special moments happen.

When I worked at Syracuse, we started a relationship with Fort Drum to bring hundreds of soldiers to a military appreciation game. It was really moving to see the impact that event had and how much it meant to everyone who participated. One of the gentlemen I worked with to get that program rolling had a nephew that had been paralyzed in a football accident, so we had the Syracuse football team visit his nephew. I'm still in touch with that gentlemen today and it's a relationship I truly cherish.

During the 2016 football season at Utah, we recognized two police officers who help our athletic department at all of our games. Being able to recognize them out on the field and thank them for keeping us safe was really powerful for us and our fans, especially with the climate of the past year. It was a great opportunity to concentrate on the good things the police force does for the community and recognize that publicly.

We also had a game where we focused on a former player who lost his son to a brain tumor this year. We were able to get him up on the video board to talk about childhood cancer and the impact his son had on our community. It was a difficult thing to do and it was a little uncomfortable for a lot of people, but it's something we felt like we needed to do for him and for all the others who are out there fighting terrible diseases. If we were able to get one person to do something that makes a difference as a result, then it was a success.

To me, the greatest moments in athletics are moments like that. It's about creating a platform that allows people to recognize and participate in something greater than themselves. It's also about moments like doing Utah's first blackout and the unbelievable experience it created for our fans, or when you never thought you could close a gift with a particular donor because everyone had already tried and then it finally happens. It all comes down to how you interact with those around you. When they're having a bad day you're able to lift them up and when you're having a bad day they're able to lift you up. Their strength is your weakness and your weakness is their strength. When you build that kind of team atmosphere and are part of that equation for others, amazing things can happen.

CHIEF WARRANT OFFICER RYAN OTTO

• • • • • • •

JASON DENNARD
*Associate Athletic Director
for Marketing and New Revenue*
Florida State University

We were fortunate to have a home game on Veteran's Day this year. It was the first Friday night football game in our history and I knew we needed to do something significant because we were the only game happening on Veteran's Day in the entire country. For the past two years, we had been talking about trying to do one of those reunions where a service member surprises their family. This game gave us the perfect opportunity to do that.

We were able to make a connection with Chief Warrant Officer Ryan Otto, a Black Hawk helicopter pilot whose wife, Jennifer, had gone to FSU. Ryan was deployed to Afghanistan from Fort Rucker, Alabama and hadn't been home in over a year. The family has four children, the youngest of whom had been born right before Ryan left. Ryan gave us a couple of different options for weekends that he might be able to make it back and it just so happened one of them was on Veteran's Day. When we made the arrangements for Jennifer and the kids to come into town for the game, we just told her we wanted to recognize her as the spouse of a deployed soldier. Ironically, we ended up putting Ryan and Jennifer up separately at the same hotel but luckily we were able to make sure they didn't cross paths.

During one of the breaks in the game, we brought Jennifer and the children out onto the field to honor the sacrifices the family had made. We were still keeping Ryan's presence secret at that point, so we made sure the announcement didn't give anything away. Then our announcer says, *Now we have a special message from your husband who recorded it all the way from Afghanistan,* which was not a lie. The video comes on of him talking, and everybody in the stands is losing it. Seeing him on that screen in that environment and hearing him tell his family how much he loved and missed them was so powerful and so emotional. Everybody – fans, coaches, players, staff – was glued to the screen.

At that point, we actually had Ryan on the sideline right near our players. And I'll never forget it: as the video's running, our star player Dalvin Cook looks over from where he's sitting on the bench and sees Ryan standing there and he's like, *You're that guy. You're that guy! You're that guy!!* Then the video ends with Ryan saying, *I'll be seeing you really soon.* As the crowd is on its feet giving Jennifer a standing ovation, Ryan takes off in a full sprint across the field toward his family. He probably ran a 4.3 40 in full fatigues! The 83,000 people in the stands were losing their minds, cheering and crying and smiling all at the same time. Cameras were focused on the Otto family so you could see it all up on the big screen: the kids crying as they watched the video, dad running toward the family, mom in shock and then the overwhelming emotion of seeing them embrace after being apart for so long. It was just incredible! The crowd started chanting, *USA! USA!* With everybody coming together in support of this family and this one single cause, it was a truly moving moment. We had already had a sponsor donate a really nice set of diamond earrings for Ryan to give to Jennifer, and as their reunion was being broadcast my phone started blowing up with text messages from others who wanted to do something because they were so moved by what they had seen.

It was a really special moment and the coolest thing we'd ever done by a long shot. About three weeks later, the Otto family stopped in to visit us and say thank you as they were driving to Disney World. Ryan presented us with a folded American flag that had been flown over the barracks in Afghanistan, along with an official proclamation letter thanking us for supporting the Army and bringing attention to the military in such a positive way. That was really neat, but I don't think anything will ever compare to how great it felt seeing him reunite with his family on that football field. It was truly one of those once-in-a-lifetime experiences for all of us, and I'm just glad we were able to make it happen.

BANNER YET WAVE

• • • • • • •

NICK KONAWALIK
Associate Athletic Director for Marketing
University of North Carolina at Charlotte

One of the best experiences that I've had as an administrator was when we kicked off the University of North Carolina at Charlotte football program. We played our very first game on August 31st, 2013 against Campbell University at the newly opened Jerry Richardson Stadium in Charlotte.

I basically had carte blanche to do what I wanted in preparing for the events so I got one of those giant American flags that literally covers the field from end zone-to-end zone and sideline-to-sideline. We solicited about 250 people including season ticket holders, military personnel and some local police officers to carry the flag out onto the field on game day. The flag comes in multiple pieces so these people actually had to be trained on how to carry it out onto the field. It was that big. I couldn't wait to see it on display the day of the game.

The stands were packed with a sell-out crowd come game time. Chelsea Sorrell, a former "American Idol" contestant, sang the National Anthem and as she got to, *Oh say! Does that star-spangled banner yet wave,* everybody holding the flag unexpectedly started waving it up and down. The crowd loved it! At that moment, it was more than just a sense of patriotism; it was a feeling that we were doing something historic together. That moment gave me chills.

We had set up pyrotechnics in the end zone, so fireworks were going off as our team ran out of the tunnel followed by our mascot, Norm the Niner. The players were either carrying an American flag, a North Carolina state flag, or our own 49ers flag as they ran out. The crowd was going wild. They were so excited to finally have a football program and you could feel and see the excitement everywhere that day. On the second play of the game, one of our players, Mark Hogan, picked off the ball and ran it back for the very first touchdown in school history. Mark had transferred to play with us his senior year after having started his college football career at Georgia State the year they launched their football program. It was really cool to think this kid had started and ended his college playing career with brand-new teams.

The stadium was unbelievably loud throughout the game. No one really knew what to expect with it being our very first game ever but there was so much excitement and everyone was so supportive of our team. We ended up dominating the game, running away with a 52-7 victory. As the game ended, our students stormed the field. It was an incredible start to the football program, from the emotional impact of the flag waving, to the scoring of the first touchdown, getting our first win and then watching the students celebrate. It's an experience I will never forget.

LIFT AS WE CLIMB

• • • • • • •

JAMAAL WALTON

Associate Athletics Director for External Operations
College of Charleston

I grew up in Virginia Beach, Virginia as part of a hardworking middle-class family. My dad played football in high school and was offered a grant to go to William and Mary College, but he decided to stay home and work instead. When I was a kid, my dad was the rec coach that everyone in town knew and my mom was always the team mom. They were always involved in the community and taught us from a young age how important it is to give back.

I remember days my father would drive 45 minutes to pick up a kid because the kid's parents couldn't get them to practice. Riding in the car at age 10 or 11 I used to think, *Man, my dad's picking this kid up every time. Why is he doing this?* As I got older, I realized, *My dad is going out of his way for these kids because they're not as lucky as I am. Some people don't have a father or a family that really cares about them and can take the time to support them.*

There was a kid named Shay'Quan Pittman who told me he wanted to play on our football team, but the weight limit was 120 pounds and he weighed closer to 130. I told my dad about it and he worked with Shay'Quan to help him get his weight down. Shay and I ended up playing together in the City Championship against a rival team that a bunch of my friends were on. Watching my dad take the extra time to help Shay taught me a lot. My parents also took in a kid named Malcolm who played sports with my older brother. I don't remember Malcolm's circumstances, but my parents let him live with us so he would have a roof over his head and meals to eat. That's just how they were and that's the example they've always set for me and my siblings. Even today when I talk to my parents, they ask me things like, *How is Shay doing? Do you remember when we used to take him with us?* In my family, the power of sports is in the memories we share and the ways we've helped other people.

The greatest thing sports has taught me is that we've got to lift as we climb. As my father was climbing up and doing some great things in the community with football championships and basketball championships, he was lifting other people up too. He went out of his way to ensure kids who didn't have a lot were able to take advantage of the opportunities sports offers, and my mom went out of her way to provide meals for kids so they could have something in their belly.

That's really when I've witnessed how powerful sports can be. It's about understanding that team effort doesn't just take place on the field and help-ing people who may not be as fortunate as you without asking for anything in return. It's about realizing that sometimes you have to take a few extra steps on your own journey to create opportunities for others, and hopefully the person you helped looks around one day and says, *You know what? I need to do the same thing for somebody else.*

BRINGING IT FULL CIRCLE

• • • • • • •

HUNTER YURACHEK
Vice President and Director of Athletics
University of Houston

College athletics is about so much more than we make it out to be as administrators. We're always talking about the bottom line and producing revenue and building great facilities, but I think we sometimes lose sight of the fact that we're educating young men and women. We're preparing them not only to get degrees and jobs, but also to become great citizens in their communities.

At the University of Houston, one of the ways we try to keep that broader focus is by having each of our teams partner with a community group. Through that initiative, our Men's Basketball team has developed an ongoing relationship with the Down Syndrome Association of Houston. In early fall of this year, before we'd gotten into the real crux of our season, we held a special basketball clinic for them at our practice facility. We gave them jerseys, and our players had lunch with them and signed autographs. As part of that initiative, we also invited them to be our guests at a game and participate in the halftime.

When the Down Syndrome Association of Houston came to our game in late January, there were probably 20 to 25 kids and adults in their group. They all wore their jerseys and they were just so excited to be there. They cheered like none of our fans had ever cheered before! When we brought them down onto the court at halftime, their smiles were unbelievable. We held their own game for them and it was one of the most touching halftime performances I've seen in a long, long time. They shared the ball and made sure each person made a shot, and they celebrated on that court like nothing I'd ever seen before! Their enthusiasm was contagious, and each time one of them made a shot our fans went crazy cheering them on. Seeing the looks of pure joy on the faces of those boys, girls, young men and young women was really moving. It was equally moving to look around at our fans and see how special a moment it was for them to watch that group play. After the game, our student-athletes and Coach Sampson came out on the court to congratulate the group and take pictures together. It was really neat to see the bond our student-athletes had formed with those kids.

Afterward, the mother of one of the participants wrote me a note thanking us for allowing her daughter to come out on our court. She talked about what an impact our team had on her daughter. To me, being able to create those types of experiences for our student-athletes, our community, and our fans is really important. I feel like that moment brought it all full-circle: how fortunate so many of us are and how we can make such a difference in another person's life by simply sharing something we might take for granted.

(14)
CHAPTER FOURTEEN
A LEVEL
PLAYING FIELD

Sport can create hope where there was once only despair. It is more powerful than government in breaking down racial barriers. It laughs in the face of all types of discrimination.
- Nelson Mandela

Guthrie is a small town of about 10,000 people located 30 minutes north of Oklahoma City, right along Interstate 35. It was actually the first capital of the state of Oklahoma and is the home of the state's first Capitol building. But in 1910, only three years after Oklahoma became a state, those scoundrels from Oklahoma City began a campaign to relocate the state capital to the much larger and economically flourishing city and by February of 1911, Guthrie was just another small town in Oklahoma.

Just west of the railroad tracks, near the Cottonwood Creek, there is an area known as the flats. Every spring when I was a kid and Oklahoma had its big storms, the creek got out and many of the houses in that area were under water. The property values there were low, obviously, and the socio-economic makeup of its inhabitants was below average as well. Like most towns, Guthrie has a few "poor" areas. The flats was definitely one of them.

I couldn't have been more than 4 or 5 years old when my big brother was playing pee-wee league football in Guthrie. My dad was the coach and as far as I was concerned, he and my brother were the most talented coach/quarterback duo in the country. In Guthrie, nearly every boy from every background played football. We lived on a farm west of town so in order to get to practice, we had to drive straight through the flats to get to there. We'd pile in the Suburban with me and the equipment in the far back (no seatbelt of course) and room for at least 5-6 more kids in the other seats. We'd head to town and then slowly wind our way through this area, stopping in front of one house after another while one more kid would run out of their house and hop in the car with us: Kevin, Danté, Elton and "Burnin'" Herman Owens. One by one we'd fill up with kids, head to practice and then take them all back home afterward.

For a lot of these kids, we were their only way of getting to practice. They didn't have the financial opportunities a lot of us did, but to that little boy in the very back, they were the greatest football players on earth. I didn't see them as black or white or rich or poor. They were all just football players and I wanted to be like every single one of them.

We hear the term *leveling the playing field* a lot, which means giving everyone in a given situation the same benefits as everyone else. The term alludes to the idea that if you played a game on a sloped field, the team moving downhill would have the advantage. On a level playing field, everyone is equal. I find it quite fitting then that sports is the one thing that above all else, puts every participant on equal footing, regardless of race, religion or socioeconomic background. Truly one of, if not *the* only place in the world, where everyone is on a level playing field, is on a level playing field.

There were so many things that divided us as children growing up in Guthrie, just as there are so many things that continue to divide us today. Our household income, the color of our skin, what part of town we live in and what religion we subscribe to all contribute to the walls that separate us. But as Chris Del Conte points out in his story, sports is *the ultimate equalizer.* Once we walk onto that field or step onto that court, the only thing that matters is how good we are. Sports connects people that, because of their backgrounds, would never have even met, much less been put in a position to rely on one another to achieve a common goal. Sports gives opportunities to individuals based solely on their athletic ability with a complete disregard for how they look or how big of a house they grew up in.

The stories in this final chapter confirm Mandela's statement that sports laughs in the face of discrimination. When I heard each one for the first time, it made me look at sports in a way I had never considered. I had experienced it, but my eyes had never been opened to the power sports has to promote equality. I believe that sports does have more power than government in breaking down racial barriers and we see thousands of examples of this throughout sports history. Sports doesn't care what color your skin is, what church you go to or where you grew up. Sports only cares about how talented you are, how hard you'll fight and how you'll respond when it tests your limits.

THE ULTIMATE EQUALIZER

• • • • • • •

CHRIS DEL CONTE
Director of Intercollegiate Athletics
Texas Christian University

I grew up in a children's home about 30 miles outside of Taos, New Mexico. There were 85 kids at the ranch, and every year we'd get five or six more kids coming in, five or six leaving. I was in it my entire life, because my father ran the children's home as a lifelong missionary and he had us live with the rest of the kids. There were 25 of us in each house: 0-to-6 in one house, 6-to-13 in another, and 13-to-18 in the oldest house. At the beginning of the school year, he'd buy us each five pair of pants, two pair of shoes, shirts, underwear, the whole bit. We'd get a new outfit for Christmas and for Easter. He'd always tell us, *You know what? You're going to be judged on how you look. Make sure you look your best. Be clean every day.* But as a kid from the ranch, acceptance was hard no matter what we looked like. Whenever we'd go into town for school or anything else, people would judge us and we'd always get teased. Sometimes being in a children's home, it's hard to see the light at the end of the tunnel.

When I was in 5th grade, something happened that changed my life. It was 1978, and two of the kids from the ranch, Vince Lauricella and Larry Platero, went out for the football team. It turned out they could play pretty well, and instantly they were accepted by the community for their exploits on the field. Suddenly, kids from town were calling out to the ranch, wanting to talk to them. Guys from school would come out to pick them up in their car. They started sitting in the back of the bus with the pretty girls. They got prom dates! I remember seeing Larry Platero coming home off the bus, carrying his shoulder pads with his helmet in there, and thinking, *My God dude, I want to be just like Larry.* When I'd go to Friday night lights and see Vince Lauricella get a big tackle, the place would go wild cheering and I'd dream of being him.

My dad sat us down and looked at all of us and said, *You know what? Sports will help you socialize more and be more accepted in the community.* And that's all that he was striving for, was to make sure that we felt accepted in the community. He wasn't into athletics but he could see the opportunities it created. After Larry Platero started playing, my dad decided: *We're all doing it, every one of you guys. Let's go.* The next day, all 85 of us were playing sports. My dad had no clue what he was doing or what we were doing, but he put us on the buses and dropped us off and said, *Get out there.*

With sports, all of a sudden we had a sense of value; we had a sense of belonging. The townspeople loved us. It didn't matter that maybe that one didn't have parents or that we were at the ranch; they knew us for what we could do on the field and they accepted us for that. Sports opened up doors that we never thought possible. That was the most revealing experience for me, and it made me love sports. We didn't have television out there, but we would read about the big teams. On the playground, I'd pretend to be different players and went from Roger the Dodger to Julius Irving to Greg Nettles. I played sports all through high school and made tons of friends that way.

I played a sport every season; we all did. My first love was football, my second love was basketball, and track was a necessity because the only other spring sport was baseball, and I'd given up on baseball after a curve ball hit me in the nose and knocked me out. I became a high jumper, and track is what ended up giving me the chance to go to Oregon State. I'm forever grateful for that opportunity. Unfortunately, while I was at Oregon State they dropped their track team because of Title IX, so I transferred to Santa Barbara to continue competing in track and finish my degree. Those sports program cuts were absolutely crushing for the kids who were affected, and I experienced that pain personally.

When it was time for me to graduate and get a job, my dad asked me, *What are you going to do?* My little brother was working for the United Nations and my entire family is in service industries – the service of humanity.

I said, *Dad, I think I'm going to go into collegiate athletics.* He asked, *Why?* I told him, *I think it's the ultimate equalizer.*

People get into sports for a variety of different reasons. For me, it was never about the competition; it was about what sports does for people and how it changes lives. If you don't dress correctly or look a certain way, you can be teased, picked on or ostracized. Sports provides anyone an avenue to overcome all of that. It has played a huge role in the transformation of our society. Just look at Jesse Owens, Wilma Rudolph, Muhammad Ali, Billie Jean King, or the football game in Alabama when Paul "Bear" Bryant made that phone call to John McKay at USC - *Come play me, I can't integrate my football team.* I got into athletics not just because of the foundation and acceptance it gave me personally, but because of what it has done for countless others. Sports gave them an opportunity to excel beyond their circumstances. I know that sports is what you do, not who you are. But what you do gives you an opportunity to fully become who you are through education. That's why I'm in it.

My father was always saying to us: *You'll be humble, you'll be honest, and you'll serve others.* That was his constant mantra: *be humble, be honest, serve others.* He gave back to humanity and taught me things I never thought possible at a young age. Growing up at the ranch, I learned compassion; I learned humility; I learned how to love. Because of how he raised me, I got to see firsthand the effects sports can have on somebody. I felt that was a worthy calling, that the ultimate sacrifice is serving others through sports. And I still firmly believe it today.

When I was graduating from Santa Barbara, a man named Dr. Donati who had been a house parent at the ranch was the team doctor at Washington State University. He called the AD and got me a job in the maintenance department. And me, I just worked my way up from there. But the reality is, it all started at the ranch and what sports did for all of the kids.

SMALL WORLD

• • • • • • •

PEG BRADLEY-DOPPES
Vice Chancellor of Athletics and Recreation
University of Denver

I grew up as one of nine children: eight girls, one boy. Today I would have been considered a hyperactive child, but back then they just called me precocious and my parents let me play outside a lot so I could blow off steam. In grade school I played every sport there was and even punted with the practice football team. When I was in high school I played volleyball, basketball, softball, track, tennis. I was fortunate enough to get a volleyball scholarship and played volleyball collegiately for four years; I also ran track and played two years of basketball.

After graduating from college, I played with the American Express IDS U.S. Volleyball Association and had the unique opportunity to study, train, and compete in the Soviet Union. That was in 1979, when the Cold War was at its height and the USSR was still the great unknown. The only way we were able to go was through a treaty with Trudeau and the Canadian government. I was one of 50 North American athletes to participate in the program; 48 of them were male athletes from the national teams for wrestling and track and field.

At the time Moscow was preparing for the 1980 Olympics, which the U.S. later boycotted. Being able to go over there during the train-up period and experience their culture was incredible. When we went to the Red Army Sports Camp they took away our passports because they were considered diplomatic. We stayed in the dormitories that the athletes trained in and we were given incredible opportunities like seeing the Bolshoi, going to the front of the Lenin Tomb and visiting a religious community maybe 45 miles away from Moscow. We weren't able to converse with the Soviet athletes, but the language of sport helped us transcend the barriers between us. For someone as young and as sheltered as I was at the time, it was absolutely amazing to be there.

We had an interpreter named Nina who had recently gotten married. Her husband was multilingual too but he was considered a distraction so they actually sent him away to help Nina concentrate on us. She may have spoken several languages but the fascinating thing to me was how shocked she was that the two sets of athletes were so similar despite our differences. We shared a love of competing at the highest level and a desire to strive for excellence, and sports unified us in a way no other experience could have.

Back then the currency wasn't money, it was U.S. items like Levi's jeans, Bic pens, and chocolate candy bars. Snickers bars were like gold currency, they could get you anything! The big department store at St. Basil's Square had nothing on the shelves. Seeing how they lived and their appreciation for things we took for granted really opened my eyes. When I left to go home to the U.S., I gave Nina most of the clothes I had brought with me because I knew it would make a huge difference for her.

Through sport I've gotten to see the world and experience different cultures. It has helped me appreciate both our uniqueness and our similarities. I've always felt very blessed and fortunate to be given those opportunities and it has instilled in me a sense of obligation to give my best and fullest in return. As both an athlete and as an administrator, I've seen athletics make the world so much smaller. It's a unifier that brings people together to cheer or commiserate, to dream and to aspire. From the beauty of high-level athletic ability to the grit of the 85-year-old that's still running a mile or riding a bike, sports is a microcosm of what makes humans so special.

FAST FRIENDS

• • • • • • •

BOB ROLLER
Director of Athletics
Campbell University

One of the most amazing aspects about athletics is how it brings people from different backgrounds together. Individuals of varying upbringings are able to form lifelong friendships through college athletics. One day they do not know each other and the next they are placed on the same team. I see it happen frequently at Campbell University. Our athletics program brings students to our campus from states throughout the country and many foreign nations. Watching these young men and women learn from each other and find common ground is one of the greatest aspects of my job.

There was one such friendship that truly stands out in my career. It was a friendship between two basketball players who enrolled at Samford University in Birmingham, AL where I was the director of athletics for 11 years. Jim Griffin was an Irish-Catholic young man from the south side of Chicago playing in the Catholic Young Leagues. Jim was the kind of guy everyone gravitated toward. He and I had an unspoken habit of giving each other a fist-bump whenever we saw each other on campus. Trey Montgomery was an African-American student from rural Destrehan, LA outside of New Orleans. The two arrived on campus the same summer with very few similarities within their first 18 years of life. However, over the next three years they forged a friendship that continues to leave a legacy from Louisiana to Birmingham to Chicago. The two redshirted their first year and then played three seasons together for Samford. They were roommates who became close friends. Jim and Trey were like brothers.

In the fall of their senior season, Jim did not wake up one morning as his alarm went off. Trey thought it was a joke as the two often pranked one another. But that morning it was not a prank. Jim was not breathing. Trey attempted to revive him and called for help, but it was too late. Jim had died during the night from unknown causes (later determined as a heart ailment). It devastated the entire Samford community, but no one more than his best friend, Trey. Later in the week, Trey delivered the eulogy at Jim's funeral in Chicago and it was the most unbelievably moving tribute I've ever heard. The Griffin and Montgomery families remain close to this day.

When you work in intercollegiate athletics, the kids become like your sons and daughters in a way. You try to be there for them, not just for the free throws or the soccer matches, but also for their struggles and their day-to-day lives. It becomes a family and, within that family, a lot of the kids on the teams will form lifelong friendships like Jim and Trey. You watch different races, socio-economic backgrounds, and geographic boundaries dissolve as they form unshakeable bonds. It's a privilege to work in this environment and watch athletics bring people together.

EXTRA POINTS

In November of 2016, I set out to write a book focused on exciting sports stories provided by a handful of athletics administrators. I didn't go into it thinking I'd change anyone's perspective or opinion on sports. However, my journey took me down an entirely different path than I'd planned and I'll be forever changed and grateful for that detour.

I found that when asked to provide a story demonstrating the power and impact sports can have, the responses were far different than I anticipated. Plenty told me stories about big wins and dramatic finishes, which we all love reading because those moments are what make sports so exciting. But the majority of the stories had much more to do with how sports shapes our lives. Their stories prove that sports is far more than just exciting. It's important.

What started as a book of thrilling stories intended to entertain became a book of meaningful and poignant stories intended to make people think. I thought I was writing a book that people would want to read. I ended up with a book people need to read. Whether you're a sports fan or not, we can all benefit from the lessons presented in this book. If you're a coach, I hope this book helped you fully understand the impact you can have on your athletes. If you're an athlete, I hope you have a new understanding of not only how sports shapes your own life but how you affect others' lives as well. As for administrators, I hope this book provided you with some guiding principles that will positively affect the way you think about your job.

Athletics connects people of all races, religions and backgrounds like nothing else in the world. It heals emotional wounds and creates memories that stay with people throughout their lives. Athletics provides futures for those without hope. It changes us, defines us and reveals us. It makes us better. If not for athletics, we would never experience so many things we currently take for granted.

If not for athletics, the incredible events in these stories, and thousands like them, would not be possible.

THANK YOU

This book would not have been possible if not for the contributions of so many people. My most sincere and heartfelt gratitude goes out to all of them for their role in helping me make this book happen.

First and foremost, to my wife Holli. You are not only the most amazing woman I've ever met and the love of my life, you also gave me the confidence and support I needed to take on this project. You listened every night as I told you about the stories I'd heard that day from contributors to this book and you read every single page multiple times to make sure it is as good as it could possibly be. The many ways in which you improved this book and improve my life cannot be overstated.

To my sons, Zye and Tace, for allowing me the opportunity to coach you, take you to sporting events and for playing baseball with me in that empty field by our house. I love you more than you could ever know.

To my stepdaughters, Mabry and Carlee, for giving me the chance to have the daughter I always wanted, times two. You have enriched my life beyond belief.

To my father, who named me after a Sooner football player and laid the groundwork for my love of sports, for always believing in me and for helping create some of the greatest memories of my life.

To my mother, for agreeing to name me after a Sooner football player, for always being proud of me and for encouraging my creativity.

To my business partner, Roy Page. You empowered me and encouraged me at every step and have been influential to me in so many ways. Without you, this book would undoubtedly have never happened.

To my friend and colleague, Robert Smith, who came to work for me in 2005 and without whom Old Hat would not be nearly the success it is.

To the staffs at Old Hat and Powerhouse, who supported this effort every step of the way, making it possible for me to take the time necessary to do everything one needs to do to write a book like this. They are:

Kevin Kelly, Jentry Miller, Roy Page, Natalie Powers, Robert Smith, Misty Copeland, James Cyrus, Kriste Day, Hannah Deutsch, Jessica George, Ashley Gloystein-Klatt, Elizabeth Isbill, Deb Livingston, Josie Logsdon, Megan Miranda, Joel Richardson, Geoffrey Rogers, Tricia Rogers, Dustin Schmidt, Laura Slipsky, Jared Stanley, Mark Trail and Douglas Wilson.

To Barry & Becky Switzer and Trip Durham for connecting me with many of the contributors to this book.

To Sherry Pemberton for transcribing every word of every interview I conducted.

To Zac Stevens for his editing assistance and for being a part of so many of my great sports memories.

To Travis Monroe for his editing assistance and encouragement throughout the process.

To Jennifer Havens and David Chapin for their encouragement and advice throughout the project.

To the 57 athletics administrators who were so giving of their time and so gracious in sharing a story with me for this book.

To Jared Stanley for designing no less than 20 different cover concepts before we finally landed on this one. You are one of the most talented designers I've ever known.

And finally, to Megan "The Force Multiplier" Miranda, who took every transcript of every interview, researched the people and events described and turned those conversations into the amazing stories that have filled the pages of this book. You are amazing!

Made in the USA
Middletown, DE
17 December 2017